T0209567

DON'T FORGET TO BE
LIGHT

AMELIA HOMEWOOD

WESTBOW
PRESS®
A DIVISION OF THOMAS NELSON
& ZONDERVAN

WestBow Press books may be ordered through booksellers or by contacting:

WestBow Press
A Division of Thomas Nelson & Zondervan
1663 Liberty Drive
Bloomington, IN 47403
www.westbowpress.com
844-714-3454

Scripture taken from the King James Version of the Bible.

ISBN: 978-1-6642-6435-9 (sc)
ISBN: 978-1-6642-6434-2 (hc)
ISBN: 978-1-6642-6436-6 (e)

Library of Congress Control Number: 2022906966

Print information available on the last page.

WestBow Press rev. date: 07/26/2022

For Riese.

THANK YOU FOR ALWAYS BELIEVING IN ME. I KNOW YOU
ARE ALWAYS WITH ME. UNTIL WE MEET AGAIN.

PREFACE

The title for this book was chosen with specific intent. Be light in all you do.

Be lighthearted. Walk with childlike joy. Do not let the inevitable external forces of life weigh you down. If they do, I pray you find that love and bravery deep down inside you, to start over and allow yourself to be the light of your own life again.

Let me tell you all my story.

Why should you care? Valid question.

I suppose it's open to interpretation. You will find a lot of dark things in this book—countless compound trauma, a few deaths, and an unplanned teenage pregnancy of a girl who had the world at her feet. You will also find the story of a woman who overcame countless obstacles and created a life worth living. They say we all have a story within is—our own.

Allow me to share mine with you.

I promise you will not regret reading this.

The Background

I was born into a nonconventional family. But if I am going to tell my story, I suppose I must start from the beginning.

My dad was born in Olongapo, Philippines. He was one of five siblings. They were impoverished, living in a Third World country with no promise for their future. My grandma was a single parent of four, struggling to provide for her children, and was introduced to my grandfather, a Navy SEAL based on her island.

My dad, one of the most handsome and charismatic humans you could ever meet in your lifetime, had a lot of demons. He grew up in a Third World country with limited resources. He told me stories of days when there was barely any food. He said once that he was walking past a house and was so hungry that he watched through the window as the family ate rice. These demons inevitably caused him to struggle with addiction. When I was a child, he would get drunk and talk about his past. He had a brother there still, and I know it bothered him that he never had the chance to come to America.

He used to get drunk and tell me the story of the night they left the Philippines. He said he and his siblings had been sleeping on the floor, his brother on his arm. He said to his brother, "We'll be back, okay?" Obviously, that did not happen. It was a dark demon my dad carried around for years, and I am positive he still does.

My grandma was a strong woman who would do whatever it took to get her family out of there. I cannot pretend to know why my dad's brother did not come with them. We only ever know what others choose to share with us, and my grandmother took this one with her to the grave.

My mother, a strikingly kind and beautiful woman, was born and raised in a small town that never did her any favors. A funny truth about small towns is that most of us who live in them have known the people there from the time we were children. We have seen them in most phases of their lives, and unfortunately, we know every last detail about them. At least, most people think they do. We have seen them make life-altering decisions and pubescent mistakes based on hormones and impulses. We have seen them make mistakes as children, teenagers, and adults. It is easy to assume you truly know a person based on what you have heard about them. However, that is rarely ever the case, and some small towns do not easily offer grace and acceptance when you have grown.

My mother was also raised by a single parent, who, like my father's mother, had experienced generational poverty and trauma. My parents met when my dad moved to the town from Houston, Texas. They fell into that wild teenage love when they were sixteen, and they had my sister. Four years after, I arrived. Why is this important? Because, as you can imagine, since both came from generations of unresolved issues, together, they combined to create one of the most traumatic households I have ever witnessed.

They say misery loves company, and though I would never describe my parents as miserable humans, I know they had deep sorrow between them that connected them in ways only they understood—two wonderfully mysterious humans bonded by trauma.

To summarize, I grew up in a household surrounded by addiction, trauma, and abuse. Before I go any further, let me say, this is just my story. I did not write it to highlight the negative aspects of my life (as I perceive them) but to show how I overcame numerous inevitable life-altering circumstances for the better and made the conscious effort to break multiple generational curses.

My childhood was filled with partying, drinking, drug use, and many lost souls coming together in a group that was so magnetic that they mistook their codependence for meaningful connection. I suppose some of them did have meaningful connections; only they know. However, it was not healthy. There were nights when the drinking got so bad, full-blown fistfights would erupt between my dad and his friends, my dad and other people's friends, my mom and her friends, my mom's friends and my dad's friends, random people at the bar—you name it.

I once watched five guys jump my dad in a bar parking lot and knock out his front teeth. Yes, I was at the bar with them, and at only nine years old. Sometimes, my parents would get into fights so violent, I thought one or both would end up dead. My parents had a hot-and-cold marriage most of my life. Things would be peaceful for a little while, and then something would happen, and they would split up again. We would get woken up in the middle of the night and go stay with relatives for days, sometimes weeks, before ending up back home. Other times, we did not go home and moved completely.

When I was around eight years old, one of these party fights came to its inevitable fatal conclusion, the accidental stabbing of my dad's best friend. I do not remember the details of the incident; however, I remember hearing the news and being devastated. I watched my dad, my mom, and her best friend, who had been dating this man at the time, crumble around me. This happened to be a high-profile court case in my hometown, which, thank God, resulted in a guilty conviction. My cousin Riese and I authored a short story about it, which was later featured on the news. This friend, an uncle, would be the first, but unfortunately not the last, of my life's many tragic losses.

There were times when I would be up listening to screaming, fighting, and loud music until the early hours of the morning. Then, I would go to school and pretend everything was fine. It was not fine. I was no scholar. I was always tired, anxious, and worried about what would come next. I was always smart, but I lacked the resources to focus, which success requires. Perhaps you've heard of the theory of motivation, based on Abraham Maslow's hierarchy of needs. At the bottom are basic needs such as rest, security, and safety. I did not have those. If you do not have even these basic needs met, you hardly have a foundation for success.

I have heard and read so many stories about children from toxic households. Let me tell you what makes my story peculiar. Usually, these children struggle with trauma for the rest of their lives; they are sent out to navigate this big, scary world with almost no life skills because their parents did not have them either. It is a massive generational disappointment. The moment I stopped being bitter toward my parents for all the things that happened to them and stepped back to look at the bigger picture, my life instantly changed.

They too had been subjected to difficulties. Otherwise, why would they have been this way? The difference between them and me is that I was raised in the Information Age, with access to anything I needed to know at my fingertips, via Google. To give myself a little credit, it took a lot of hard and uncomfortable work to challenge the preconceptions engrained into my mind as a child. It took many years, in fact, but I managed.

I want to pause here to acknowledge that my manner of writing this may hurt some people who have not healed. On the other hand, it may be *exactly* what some people need to hear, and that is the point of the whole book: to tell my individual truth with such raw honesty, love, and clarity that I might inspire others to do the same. I am here to heal. I pray that if anything good comes from this book, it is the understanding that *you* oversee your future. You oversee your happiness, regardless of your circumstances, but it takes forgiveness, healing, and love. So now, let's go forward.

CHAPTER ONE

Dad

As I said in the introduction my dad is one of the most charismatic people I have ever met. No, I do not just say that because he is my dad. For my entire life, anywhere we went, people stared at my dad. He had a starlike quality that immediately drew people's attention and a sense of confidence in himself and his abilities that demanded respect. Frankly, no matter what my dad did, people seemed compelled to give him forgiveness and respect. What was not talked about enough was his heart. It was not talked about enough because although his heart was such a beautiful, admirable part of him, equally big was his temper. Have you ever met someone you cannot stop rooting for, even from afar, because their raw tenacity is admirable? That was my dad. People loved him. People respected him. Even if they did not, they usually came around because he was never too proud to apologize and keep learning.

As I said, I am a first-generation American on my dad's side. He, his siblings, and my grandma all came here from the Philippines when he was nine years old. They were adopted by my grandfather, who was in the navy and had married my grandmother. After they were brought here, my grandparents had my youngest uncle. I always admired my grandfather because he was a quiet, gentle, and loving man. Many of my good childhood memories include him taking my cousins and me sledding, playing board games, and providing a safe space in his home.

My grandmother, a feisty, unstoppable force of a woman, also came from a household in the Philippines riddled with abuse. My dad would often tell me stories about his maternal grandfather, describing him as a particularly dark man. My grandma clearly developed some survival instincts and ended up here in the United States, where she made a comfortable life for herself. In my experience, though, some of that darkness followed her, something inside her that sometimes weighed her down. Other times, she was incredibly lively and funny. However, when I tell you she could have a mean streak, you'd better believe it! She was four feet ten, a hundred pounds, and not to be played with.

On my dad's side, I have two aunts, an uncle from my grandparent's marriage and an uncle in the Philippines I have never met. When I tell you I come from a big family, I mean it: on my dad's side alone, I have twelve cousins—eight here in the States and four in the Philippines. One cousin, Riese, is the basis for this story. Remember that name.

CHAPTER TWO

Mom

I wish I had the right words to describe my mom. In fact, this chapter gave me writer's block for a couple of hours. In every sense of the way, I could only describe her as a fairy. She believes in magic, she believes in light, she believes in all things. That is essential to her being. She's five feet four, with stunning teal eyes, blonde hair, and a healing essence that makes people she just met want to tell them their whole life story. Unfortunately, she also had a temper. As you might imagine, this did not go well being married to another human with an intense temper. The result was years of explosive fights, screaming, fighting, and flying fists. Add some alcohol in there, and now you had a real show.

My maternal grandmother—my Mimi, as we call her—was the mirror image of my paternal grandmother in many ways. She was another unstoppable force of a woman. She had three failed marriages to men who never treated her well, one all but skipping town in the middle of the night and leaving her over $18,000 in debt. She worked three jobs simultaneously for almost six years just to take care of her kids and pay her bills.

She would tell me stories when I would ask about that time

in her life. These stories are inspiring and motivating nowadays—waking up at 5:00 a.m., walking 4.8 miles to one job, then walking to her second job, then her third, then walking home in the winter after being on her feet all day. She came from deep Native roots and was not built for giving up.

She had been through a lot in her life, so she always had little tolerance for BS but a heart of gold. Her love language was acts of service and gift giving, so even if she did not always know exactly what to say, I could feel her support when she would call me and declare, "I made potato soup and cinnamon rolls if you want to stop by and grab them." She was an extremely hard worker, and she was loved.

She worked for the public school as a custodian for many years and was so loved and appreciated that one year, they made her grand marshal in the homecoming parade. I always loved that about her. She knew what it was like to suffer and did not want anyone around her to feel that way.

On my mom's side, I have an aunt and two uncles. My aunt and her husband would later become second parents to me. She was my first "best friend" and always made me feel safe and loved. We used to sing "Baby Girl," by Sugarland, and I would tell her that even after I became well-known, I would love her more than anything in the world. There are few people in the world like my aunt. She walks into a room, and you just want to smile. She is a breath of fresh air. She is kind, loving, emotional, and hilarious. She would be a haven for me throughout my life. She was the kind of person who, when handling my temper tantrums and fits of anger, would respond with love and kindness, which, in turn, instilled the soft, loving qualities within myself I most admire.

Her husband, my uncle, is not afraid to speak his mind. He is a hard worker, he loves hard, and he stands up for his beliefs. He is also a big softy, although he might laugh at me for saying so. As soon as I met him when I was six years old, I knew we were going to be best friends. I told my mom one day, "Can you take me to Auntie's house? I want to hang out with my friend." Sure enough, their house and that "friend" would forever become my sanctuary.

I would spend hours wrestling around with him in the kitchen, jumping on his back, and causing a ruckus in the middle of a Wal-Mart aisle. We would drive my aunt wild with that. We would go on long walks together, play basketball, and watch movies. They took me on vacations and provided me with a sense of normalcy amid the constant chaos. He would later buy me my wedding dress and walk me down the aisle alongside my father.

CHAPTER THREE

Here We Go

You now know as much about my childhood lineage as I am willing to put on paper. Remember when I mentioned the name Riese? This person was the most authentic, genuine connection I ever felt. We were first cousins, but anyone who knew us might better describe us as twins. We were five months apart in age and inseparable our entire lives.

During those parties I spoke of earlier, we would be in the back room making pretend "maps" to get us from one end of the trailer to the next without being seen. We always thought we nailed it (we did not, by the way), but it was nonetheless fun. We would play pretend for hours in our grandmother's pool. Ever seen *The Little Mermaid*? I was the princess, Ariel, and he was the fish, Flounder. I am sure he loved that. He went with it anyway because we were best friends living in the moment and just playing our hearts out.

My dad's sister was his mom, a petite woman with black hair and matching eyes and a sassy walk that still makes me laugh. She loved her family fiercely and would do anything in her power to protect them. Small but mighty, much like my grandmother, she was also a teenage mom and no stranger to struggle but loved me as her own, providing me with respite from the chaos in her home as well.

Many of my childhood years were spent away with Mimi, aunts and my uncle. Riese and I would stay awake, giggling for hours while playing *Mario Party* and watching movies. Most weekends, my aunt took us to the local supermarket where she lived, which had a movie rental station. We would pick out movies, games, and a snack. Often, we would go in the backyard and play basketball for hours. When we got sick of this, we would go jump on the trampoline until we got tired, then just lie there, talking about ridiculous things.

He still thinks Jason beat Freddy in that one horror film, but I'm still not convinced. My aunt had an old Ford sitting over by the trees. At twelve years old, there we were, getting in and pretending we were driving around, listening to "Miami" by Will Smith and "It Wasn't Me" by Shaggy, (also totally appropriate for two twelve-year-old kids, I know). These became core memories I would cherish forever. We will talk about him more later in the story. But now, it's essential to establish the correct timeline for the events that were about to change our lives.

CHAPTER FOUR

The Drowning

Think I've already told you about all my traumas? Take a seat; we are just getting started. When I was around eight years old, I was in the garage with my dad, who was filling up my bike tire. It was a crisp fall weekend, and my mom was outside doing some yard work. Although I have not yet mentioned them, I have two siblings who mean the absolute world to me: my beautiful sister and my forever-angel-on-earth little brother, who was two at the time of his accident. We will talk more about them in later chapters.

Back to the bike tire. I remember my mom walking into the garage and saying, "Where's Christian?"

My dad looked up with eyebrows arched and said, "I thought he was with you?"

At eight years old, you do not have a complete sense of how the world works, but do already have a keen sense of when you should panic. Everyone ran in different directions looking for him, and you better believe I panicked.

We lived in the country on a road that cars decided had no speed limit, so I'm sure the first thought was the road. My grandparents had ten acres of land, and we lived in a trailer that had been passed down to my parents, which was about fifty feet from my grandparents' home. This is important because while my parents ran off looking for my brother, for whatever reason, I knew exactly where to go. Call it a hunch, an intuition, divine intervention—whatever it was—I immediately went to the pool.

This pool sat at the bottom of a steep hill—why, I do not know. It seems like a chaotic design, but I am no professional. My brother was wearing a red Reebok tracksuit that day. Funny, isn't it, the things trauma makes you remember? Anyway, I stood at the top of the hill and noticed a red shape floating in the water. I am not sure how I felt at that moment because I may have blocked it out, but my instinct was to scream. I remember screaming at the top of my lungs and my dad running from behind me at full speed, jumping into the water. He pulled the limp form that was my two-year-old brother out of the pool, and I watched in sheer disbelief and agony that my baby brother's face was completely blue—no movement, no sound, just still. My dad had previously been in the army and had learned CPR, which he started to administer. Nothing, just that shrill stillness. My mom had come over and started screaming at the top of her lungs, "No, God, please! Bring him back to me! This cannot be happening!"

One thing about my parents: they loved their children. Someone shouted at my sister to call 911. I remember the paramedics showing up, but the rest of it is kind of a blur. I know he had no heartbeat, meaning he was clinically dead, but the paramedic that showed up was new and made it obvious he had no intention of giving up on my brother. He continued to administer CPR until we heard, "I got a pulse!"

A second man confirmed, "It's faint, but it's there."

I grew up in a rural community with a small hospital that happened to me less than a mile up the road from us. My brother was rushed there, and the doctors logically explained to my parents that even if he did survive, he would likely be brain dead. My mother and father refused to believe that, and my mother said, "God will not do that to me." I still remember that.

He was rushed to the Children's hospital closest to us, where he lost his pulse four more times in the helicopter. I rode with my mother and father, aunt, and one other person whom I cannot recall because, to be frank, as I stated before, I was eight, and it was a big day for all of us.

I have often been asked, what makes you believe in God? Well, moments like these next few. We got lost, the town we were headed to was quite large and the hospital was in the middle of downtown. We followed the car directly in front of us to the nearest gas station and asked for directions to the hospital. As it happens, she was a nurse there and directed us exactly where we needed to go.

My brother was in a coma for a couple of days, and they prepared my parents for the worst. I remember being showered with love—family, parents' friends, social workers, and people from our community who would send cards and say they were praying for us. This is the good part, so stay with me. By some miracle, my brother woke up. They were not exactly sure the extent of his brain damage, but he woke up with a force that left us all awestruck and started pulling at his IVs and choking on his breathing tube. When I say you could feel the collective energy, I can only explain it as catharsis: the doctor, my parents, and everyone in the room, in harmony.

Christian ended up having to relearn everything. He could not remember how to walk, talk, eat on his own—any of it. It was a long, hard journey for all of us. We had him back, and even though it was not the version of him we were used to, that was okay. It just took a lot of adjusting expectations and overcoming obstacles. And there were many. He is now twenty years old, and he still struggles with speech and basic motor function, and he is very childlike. We do not mind, though. His soul is soft and light, he was blessed by God to have a second chance at life, and all of us determined to make the best out of it.

I feel it's appropriate to pause here and recite that old cliché: "Everything happens for a reason." Have I experienced enough for you to believe that yet? If not, let's keep going.

CHAPTER FIVE

The Hot-Headed Teenager

Oh boy, this was a doozy. If you want to talk about cliques, try growing up in a small rural town. A bunch of hormonal teenagers stumbling around being friends one minute and mad at each other the next. Typical high school stuff, right? Still, high school is traumatic for us all. It is incredibly difficult. You are too young to be treated like an adult and too old to be making childish mistakes. However, in life, you only learn from mistakes. More than that— you learn best from mistakes if they are met with compassion and forgiveness. My high-school experience comes with lots of baggage, and rest assured, I play a part in the negative stories of others. (See chapters 1 through 4 and do some research on intense compound and unresolved trauma.) I discovered I inherited that hot head both my parents had. Surprise, right?

Doing some self-reflection these last few years, I want to write this chapter with as much honesty as possible but also with grace. Now, as an adult, people would tell me I am quite hard on myself. I was kind and loving to people as well. I guess it all comes down to perspective. As I said, I am sure I am still the villain in some stories. I suppose we all have been at one point or another.

I was angry most of the time, which I thought everyone knew. Oddly, many people had a different perspective on me. Anyway, back to the point. I became mischievous. I got in some legal trouble. I had a lot of arguments with a lot of people. I fell in love with the star athlete. For a moment, I found happiness and calm. And then I got pregnant.

I remember thinking something was wrong. To be completely honest, I thought I was dying. I had a splitting headache that wouldn't go away, excessive puking, and stomach cramps like you wouldn't believe. Ever met a hypochondriac? Hi, allow me to introduce another feature of Amelia. I was a severe hypochondriac when I was a teenager. Therefore, in my mind, I clearly had a brain tumor. Google and WebMD confirmed it. I made a doctor appointment immediately. When I got there and told my doctor everything, she said, "Is there any chance you could be pregnant?"

"Well ... no. I'm eighteen! I mean ... technically, yes. But there is no way. That would not happen to me."

She looked at me kindly and said, "Well, how about we run some tests and see what comes up? We'll start with a urinalysis."

So that's where we started. That's also where we ended. The test was positive.

The doctor came into the room, shut the door gingerly behind her, and in my gut, I knew what that meant. I wish I could recall the next few moments of that defining moment in my life, but I can't. The ironic part about life is that some of our most defining moments are shuffled by our consciousness out of sight. Our body keeps score—we remember the pain, the excitement, the love, whatever feeling was attached—but the exact sequence of events seems to shift. Mostly, I just remember feeling my feet and my fingertips suddenly going cold and white. I remember the headache I hadn't been able to get rid of for a week was instantly gone. Instead, I felt immense fear, frustration, shame, and honestly, the need to hurl.

My boyfriend had just gone off to college to wrestle and find his place in the world. I was a senior in high school with split-up parents who hadn't even found their own path in life. I was devastated. I swore I was getting out of that town, and now, all I could see was being stuck in the same situation faced by generations before me. I didn't want to call my boyfriend; I didn't want to be responsible for ruining his life. I didn't want to call my parents or my aunt and uncle. They had expectations of me. I was smart. I was driven. They would be so disappointed. I just got in my car and found myself at my best friend's house. When she opened the door, I immediately started crying.

CHAPTER SIX

The Inspiring Best Friend

Before I go on, let me tell you another fun fact. (How many fun facts are there in this book? Probably a lot.) My best friend and I have been attached since we were about ten years old. It was one of those connections where you meet someone for the first time and you just know you'll always want them in your life. She was tall, beautiful, funny, lighthearted, and literally the smartest human I had ever met. I was always inspired by her brain. She was also a teenage mother. My nephew was born the month after she turned seventeen. At this point in her life, she had finished the remainder of her high school career online via Penn State and had a place with her dad, where I knew I would be met with love, respect, and no judgment.

When I got there and told her, she looked shocked. She told me that it was hard, but it could be done. I told her I was scared and sad because I had so many dreams and aspirations that I was certain wouldn't come to fruition now. We talked for several hours. We sat in the living room, letting the conversation fly, wondering where our paths would take us. Uncertain of the future, unable to change the past, we were just two young people heading down what would be a long, winding road of hardship (little did we know how hard, at the risk of foreshadowing).

Interestingly, that day, she told me all about her dreams to become a pharmacist; it seemed like such a faraway goal at that time, but she was sure she could do it. She told me she always knew I had a creative mind. Maybe one day, I would write a book about all the events of my life. I remember leaving the conversation feeling better about the situation. Then I remembered I still had to call my boyfriend. Instant anxiety.

My best friend would go on to finish her degree, and she is now in the process of becoming a pharmacist. She beat the odds, experiencing a stroke (due to a blood clot on the brain) and a premature pregnancy (her second child, born at thirty-one weeks due to underlying health complications). By the grace of God, both mother and child made it through alive and well. My niece was born breathing and crying on her own at thirty-one weeks old. I am inspired every day by her tenacity.

CHAPTER SEVEN

The Boyfriend

For the sake of privacy, we'll call the person in question "Spencer." I mentioned earlier that Spencer was a star athlete. As ironic as it sounds, that was the least interesting thing about him. If I could put a metaphor to it, I would say he paved a path of kindness everywhere he went. I met him briefly a couple of months before we started dating, at a Halloween party that Riese, my best friend, and I threw. I remember him walking into the room. He was magnetic, quiet but smiley.

He wasn't there long, and we didn't talk that night, but I always remembered the feeling I got from him. Shortly after, we met in the high school cafeteria. I mentioned earlier that he was an athlete. Spencer was a state-placing wrestling prodigy who everyone knew was going places. Did I mention he was also really smart? I'm talking salutatorian intelligence.

Back to the story. If you know anything about wrestling, you know wrestlers have to cut weight to compete in their weight class. Well, that day after lunch, while we were sitting outside the cafeteria with some friends, I said, "Does anyone want my carrots?" He looked up like the carrots were a chocolate cake drizzled in all his favorite toppings. I was so confused, but I laughed and said, "Do you want them?" Romantic, right? We still laugh about it because I didn't know he couldn't even have the carrots despite the fact he hadn't eaten all day. Whoops!

We dated on and off for the remainder of high school, and I was heartbroken when he left for college. I was a year younger than Spencer, so I knew I would have to endure my last year of high school without him. My best friend had decided two years earlier that homeschooling was more her accurately her path in life. Most of my close friends had graduated the same year as Spencer, and because of my inability to hold my tongue when I got mad, accompanied by a partying habit I had developed at this time—we usually end up repeating behaviors modeled to us, don't we?—I had to spend my last year completing high school alone. I didn't have the easiest time making friends with the girls in my grade.

We broke up for a little while for the summer because back then, expressing my emotions in a healthy way wasn't a tool in my tool box. Instead, I just broke up with him.

We kept in close contact and remained close friends. He, Riese (my best friend), and I had developed such a close bond. They both kept telling me they didn't understand why I went about things the way I did. And one day, it hit me: I didn't understand, either.

My cousin, Riese (more like my twin, as I mentioned earlier), said something that still sticks with me today. "You know, it's okay to let people love you, man. It's all right."

This was one of the last weekends of the summer. Riese and I had gone on a two-mile walk, just talking about all the things we'd been through in our short lives, trying to figure out where we kept going wrong. He encouraged me to let people see who I really was instead of putting on a facade so I didn't get hurt by external situations and people.

Later that night, I impulsively called Spencer, hoping he would pick up, which he did.

"What are you doing tonight?" I said "I'm going to drive to you."

He lived about an hour and a half away and had no idea what I was thinking.

He replied, "It'll be almost ten o'clock by the time you get here." I didn't care. I just knew I had to go. He let out a slight exhale/giggle and said, "I'll see you soon then."

We got back together at the end of the summer, and in the last semester of my senior year, I ended up pregnant.

After I left my best friend's house, telling her the news, I knew I had to call Spencer. Few people in my life loved me unconditionally. Spencer was one of them. I wasn't afraid to call him because I thought that would change. I was afraid to call him because the thought of things changing between us terrified me. Would I become an obligation now? Somebody he had to stay and settle with because he got her pregnant in high school? What would his parents say?

I hadn't experienced unconditional love in a romantic relationship before. He was my first real love, and now, I was afraid to question the intent of the relationship. I bit the bullet and made the phone call in the car. The response was dead silence.

Then, very sweetly, he said, "Okay, can I call you back?"

Processing.

He called me back a few hours later. "I cleaned my whole apartment." (Imagine four college-aged wrestlers living together, and you can picture how long that would have taken). "I'm coming home tonight."

CHAPTER EIGHT

The Baby

Given that presently, my son is only nine years old and unable to understand the concept that I'm writing a book about our life, I will respect his privacy, and we'll call him "Aaron." Given that Spencer and I were still kids ourselves and far from established, his parents took us in, and we lived with them throughout my pregnancy. During this time, I learned some valuable lessons about a healthy functioning family unit.

His parents took me in and loved me as their own. We had been dating on and off for about four years, so they knew me pretty well, but given the circumstances, I wasn't sure how they would react. I'll just say I severely underestimated their kindness. They nurtured me. They helped us through the pregnancy. They gave us a safe environment to thrive until we had the baby and got on our feet. If you're reading this, you played a big part in who I am today, and I will be thankful for you until my last day on earth.

Aaron was born in November 2013 and changed my life in ways that still leave me in awe. I knew from that moment, everything had to be done in his best interest. I would protect him from all harm and teach him all the lessons I had learned. (Spoiler alert: I had *many* more lessons to learn.) He was a little blond-haired, bright-blue-eyed, porcelain-skinned boy, which surprised me. With my olive skin, dark brown hair, and brown eyes, I thought I would win the genetic battle against his dad. I did not.

Have you ever seen Reese Witherspoon and her daughter? Think of that kind of cloning, and you'll have a visual of Aaron and Spencer! He was always running around the house, laughing, making a mess, causing mischief, and bringing joy to everyone on both sides of our family. We were all enamored with him.

We decided to move back an hour and a half away from our friends, family, and support system so Spencer could finish college. It took a severe toll on us. I was alone all the time, navigating life in a new city, with a new baby and no family. Spencer was gone from sunrise to sunset because he still relied on wrestling to get his scholarships and take classes. Anyone who's had a relationship filled with such hardship will know what's next. We started arguing. Things got rocky. Soon, we started not talking at all. I called my other best friend and asked her to pick me up and take me and Aaron home.

CHAPTER NINE

Alone

This chapter is called "Alone," which probably doesn't require much explanation. Given our circumstances and the dedication of both our parents, we tried to navigate balancing parenting time, breaking up in a civilized way, and finding our way in our new lives when all we had known since we were kids were each other. This did not go well for one of us. Surprise again: it was me. I hated being alone. I was miserable at what felt like the cosmic load of chaos that always ended up in my lap. I kept dropping out of college because I couldn't stand to be away from my baby. And honestly, my lack of discipline didn't help matters.

We had struggled to agree about parenting time and ended up in a whirlwind custody fight that hurt us both to our core. Neither of us wanted that. We just didn't want to be without our baby. Looking back now, we were probably fighting for the same thing. We wanted a family. We wanted to make it work, but we were too proud to sit with the mess we had made and spin our world the other way.

One of the bits of tragic irony I've come to love about life: you usually gain the tools to deal with a situation *after* the conflict has already arisen. I suppose, though, if we had all the tools to navigate this life from the beginning, we would be deprived of that sense of triumph, that feeling when we climb a steep mountain and make it to the top, that passion we feel when we leave a toxic relationship and learn to love ourselves again, that freedom of knowing that it's okay to make mistakes because mistakes are part of life and you can always make them right. These things come from a knowledge of heartache and the struggles that accompany it.

Back to the story. Our custody battle resulted in me having Aaron on weekdays and Spencer having him every weekend. At this time, we lived an hour apart, so because of school, that was the best the judge could do to make it fair to us both. I'm not sure what I was expecting. I don't think either of us would have left that courtroom satisfied about anything. It wasn't the ideal situation for either of us, but as it often does, ego prevailed.

Spencer would have been twenty-one at this time, me only twenty, with no real regard for delayed gratification. I wanted all these things for my life, and I wanted them *now*. A couple of years later, we finally sat and openly communicated through the mess we had made.

What happened next would affect my life in ways that changed me to my core. A downward spiral of events happened so quickly, I entered a fog, not reemerging until I was almost twenty-eight years old. Remember my description of substance abuse in my household? That plays a key role here.

I hated being alone. Every weekend, when I didn't have Aaron, all I did was sit and think about all the mistakes I had made to this point, all of which led where I was now: sitting in Mom's trailer, sad and alone. I am sure you can all guess what happened next: I started drinking.

Each weekend I didn't have Aaron, I would drink just so I could go to sleep without feeling the anxiety and the soul-crushing emotions running through my body. I started going to parties with people who were genuinely not good company, but the funny irony was that the older I got, the more I realized: if you have to numb your mind with any kind of substances, you are probably trying to deal with unresolved trauma. From personal experience, look out for that friend of yours who seems to be the happiest person in the room but needs alcohol to get that way.

Don't get me wrong; I'm not talking about healthy socializing. ("We've planned this girl's trip for months. We're excited and going to catch up and have some wine!") I'm no therapist, but it's possible to have a genuinely good time. I'm talking about the friend who gets blackout drunk every other weekend. Do that person a favor and make sure they are okay.

I was now making more mistakes than I had ever thought possible. Fighting with people I loved. Fighting with random strangers. Ignoring some of the people I loved most and finding myself in the company of whoever seemed to share my interests at the moment. It was dark. It was scary. But I plummeted headfirst every weekend because I couldn't stand the pain of being without my one true source of love, Aaron.

When Aaron was around, he was all that mattered. When we were together, I didn't touch a sip of alcohol. I was the best mom you could imagine. We dressed up in costumes and ran around the house. He would want to wear his Flash costume and go to the movie theater, and we would go. He'd put on his Ninja Turtles mask and want to go to the gas station to get snacks, and we would go. With him, I was the happiest, fullest version of myself. And then, every Friday, he would leave. And faithfully, every single Friday, I would cry. I would cry until I couldn't cry anymore, and then I would get something to drink or call up some friends who would go to the bar with me.

I have identified two types of people who abuse alcohol: those who need it every single day and those who drink occasionally but don't know how to stop. I was the latter. I drank with the intent of stumbling into my empty room every night and blacking out until the next morning—one day closer to Monday with Aaron. This went on for a while. After a toxic relationship, getting my car repossessed, being evicted from my apartment due to inability to pay rent, I hit rock bottom. My cousin Riese finally confronted me. Remember chapter 3? I told you he'd be essential to this story. In fact, I can't even tell you how essential he was and how often. He matched the core of my being. He knew when things weren't right, and he addressed the issue head-on.

We'll come back to that in a minute. Stay tuned.

CHAPTER TEN

Marshall

This stage of my life is as beautiful as it is painful. I've been struggling with the correct way to write this part of my story, weaving together threads of beauty and pain into a tapestry to create the perfect picture. There was plenty of both. So, let's start.

Riese had lived about an hour south of me, gone for college, and he invited me to lunch there, where we spent the day together. We watched *The Office*, one of our favorite shows, then went to Taco Bell. While we were there, he said, "Man, are you all right? You look terrible." Yes, exactly like that.

I replied, "Wow, you really know how to compliment me. Thank you so much." We laughed for a moment, and I hoped that would be the end of it. But if there's one thing about Riese, he's determined.

"Nah, seriously, though, are you okay?"

I couldn't remember the last time anyone had asked me that. I broke down right there in the middle of Taco Bell, and we both decided it might be better to finish the conversation elsewhere.

Later that night, I thought, *Whoa. I really am not okay. What am I doing with my life? Maybe I should sit at home by myself for a few months and just reflect. I could meditate and read.*

I loved to read. Reading helped me deal with all the issues that had weighed me down since childhood. Maybe I could draw and paint, a childhood hobby I'd neglected. It was a great hour-long pep talk—until the phone rang.

It was my best friend. She wanted to go do something. It was Saturday night, and some of our friends were getting together. I briefly mentioned how, being in such a dark place, I had cast out my closest friends. They, meanwhile, were elsewhere, pursuing their respective paths. During that time, my best friend had become very close with another woman—we'll call her Kathy—who, oddly enough, would become my sister-in-law. We'll come to that later in the story.

I decided I would go, but I wouldn't drink. I was on the path to mending my mistakes and improving my life so I could finish school and create my life's purpose. I worked at Rue21 as an assistant manager, which paid well enough, but I had no serious passion for it and did not see myself doing it forever.

I met my best friend at her apartment, and we got ready to go to a mutual friend's house. That's when I met Marshall (as we'll call him in this book). When Marshall walked into the room, I nearly lost my breath. He was tall, dark, and handsome—six feet four, with dark-brown eyes, black hair, and a great tan. I was immediately drawn to him.

He came over to the island we were standing at. I looked at my best friend and said, "Who is that?"

"That's my friend's brother! Remember, I told you about him?"

She had told me about him a few months earlier, but I had just gotten out of a relationship and had no interest in jumping into anything new.

I looked at him nervously. "Hi, I'm Amelia."

He looked back, smiled, and put his hand out. "Hi, I'm Marshall."

Some sparks flew for a couple of hours, and then we went our separate ways. The night ended well. I drank some water the rest of the night and ended up back home in my bed with a clear head for the first time in a long time.

I woke up the next morning and saw that I had an unread Facebook message. It was from Marshall! Talk about being giddy. I hopped out of bed and read the text. I responded, and we communicated this way for several days before he asked me to go on a date. I agreed, and we decided we would go to Applebee's. I am sure he would have taken me anywhere, but Applebee's is truly one of my favorite restaurants. Maybe it's their mozzarella sticks—who knows?

Back to the point. I never did well on first dates. They are supposed to be sublimely romantic, but my experience is quite different: sweaty palms, shaking hands, heart beating so fast I want to throw up. So, I did what anyone would do in my position: I invited eight other people. No, I am not exaggerating. I invited my best friend, her boyfriend, my cousin, her boyfriend and two of his roommates, Marshall's sister, and her husband.

Despite the crowd, it was a pleasurable night, and he laughed it off. We started hanging out on a more regular basis, moving innocent fun in to love. This had to be it. We had both gotten out of long-term relationships, were tired of doing the same ol' stuff, and were ready for something serious.

One night, some months later, we were spending time together with two of his roommates at the time; it was fun and lighthearted, living in the moment. Marshall was telling me all about his culture, things I found fascinating. He told me about his parents, his dreams of a family, and desires out of life. *Those old sparks again.* We hit it off from the second we met. I went into the room to grab something out of my bag, and he said something to me in Arabic. He was fluently bilingual. My grandmother spoke fluent Tagalog and tried to teach me, but I never really took an interest, so his language skills fascinated me. When I asked him what it meant, he said, "Will you marry me?"

(*Panics internally*).

"What?"

Let me tell you: I have never been good under pressure. I have never been great at knowing how to say no to the people I cared about, even if it was not in my best interest. At that moment, my heart knew I was not ready to get married yet, but our friends were there, and the atmosphere was vibrant. Then I thought for just one minute. Wasn't this what I had been looking for? I wanted a home, a full family. Marshall was charismatic, charming, and sweet. He cared for me, and I for him. So I said, "Yes."

The next morning, I went to my dad's house. My dad and I have always been close. For as long I could remember, regardless of all the things from my childhood, he hung over my life like the moon. He had all the qualities I could want for a best friend, with the wisdom of a man who had made plenty of his own mistakes, and he always wanted what was best for me because I was his daughter.

I remember he was doing the dishes, and I came right out with, "Dad? I think got engaged last night," almost chuckling as I said it.

He stopped what he was doing, turned around, and said, "You *think* you got engaged last night? How do you *think* you got engaged?"

Good question. I had said yes but was not entirely sure that was what I wanted so soon. I did not know much about marriage. The only one I had known had been modeled inside my own home, full of fistfights, yelling, screaming, alcohol abuse, and cheating. It was dark.

But again, this is *my* story. I love my parents. They are kind. They are loving. But they were lost, conflicted individuals doing the best with what they knew. I do not blame them for that. Life can be ugly, but the beautiful part about it is you do not have to be chained to those mistakes forever. You also do not have to chain people to their mistakes forever. They both evolved into inspiring versions of themselves. However, the truth is the truth. I had not been modeled healthy behavior for marriage and had no idea what I was doing.

I decided I would take the plunge and go through with the marriage. I had done so much work on myself up to this point and was positive I had learned from all the mistakes the people around me had made. I was now ready to make an abundantly happy life for myself. What I wanted more than anything was a family for myself and Aaron. I told myself from the day he was born that I would do anything I could to give him the life I never had. He deserved the world and more.

I was happy with Marshall. I trusted him. He had a softness that made me feel safe. I decided I would just jump headfirst, trusting my gut instinct for the first time in my life instead of talking myself out of the happiness I deserved. We had a six-month-long engagement and were married in April 2017.

As I mentioned earlier, Marshall and I would sit up all night talking about our cultures, families, and desires. Marshall had come from a Muslim family that was originally from Africa. He and his family had a rich cultural history, which I found fascinating. We had a traditional Muslim ceremony in a Masjid. It was small, just our families. Riese was my witness. He was holding my hand when I signed the marriage certificate. I could not stop shaking. I was signing my life away to marriage, thinking in my heart that I might be rushing into things. I just prayed I was finally on the right track. *Just nerves*, I thought.

This next part is important to me. After all, this is my life story, shaped by the lessons I have learned through my experiences, my pain, my happiness, my love.

I feel the need to say this: I mentioned they were Muslims, but this did not hold any significance for me at the time. I grew up in a household with an immigrant grandmother who spoke broken English. My dad was from the Philippines. I would soon realize it meant so much to other people.

To me, people are just people. You judge who you want around you by what is inside their heart, their character, their motives. Naively, I thought everyone thought this way. I learned the hard way: marry into a Muslim family, and the people around you expect you have changed. Stay with me. I know I am walking on eggshells here. But just listen. I want to talk about 9/11.

If you grew up in the US, you will understand how 9/11 is a huge part of our history. It was a defining moment where the world seemed to take a turn for the worse, and time stood still. We watched in horror as our fellow Americans lost their lives just going to work. Parents lost their children. Children lost their parents. Wives and husbands lost each other. It was a loss so deep, we will feel it until the end of time.

If you do not believe a single word you hear in your lifetime, believe what I have to say next: not all Muslims behave this way. Since it is not our culture, it was easy for many of us to be protective of our fellow Americans, judging the Islamic religion as a whole and not the individuals who commit unthinkable atrocities in the name of God.

I know these people. I love these people. Believe me when I tell you it hurt the true God-loving Muslims just as it hurt us. Marshall told me a story once about being jumped by five other boys in his middle-school parking lot. As they beat him, they called him a terrorist. My sister-in-law had her hijab ripped off just walking down the hallway at school. I want you to do something for me: Imagine the person you love the most. Do you have their image in your mind? Now imagine someone hurting them for something they had no control over. That is how I felt hearing their testimonies.

It is true: we should never forget what happened in honor of our fallen Americans, but remember, the true God-loving Muslims are just like you and me. Let us come together as one, moving forward in love so we can all heal.

Whew. That heavy weight has been sitting in my chest for a long time. So, let us just take a moment to breathe and realign.

Let us resume at the point of my marriage.

As I mentioned, we had a small traditional Islamic ceremony to honor his parents, followed by a larger ceremony four months later, to which all our friends and family came together as one. My best friends, whom I had known since childhood, stood up for me. My dad and uncle walked with me down the aisle. Aaron stood next to Marshall, and Riese conducted the ceremony. It was a defining moment in my life, when I felt genuinely excited about my next steps life. (*Spoiler alert: that bliss was short-lived*).

Our first year after getting married, things became tumultuous for Marshall and me. First, we struggled to agree on basic things. Then, we had differing opinions on what seemed like everything. To make matters worse, numerous outside forces kept interfering, causing us both pain and straining our relationship. We had friends we had to let go of during this time because their lifestyles no longer aligned with ours.

We grew closer together with each passing day, clinging to each other as the stars clung to the sky. We knew what we wanted, and we would fight for it at all costs. I started to wonder, *How long are we supposed to fight? I know it is a marriage, I know we said for life, but this is hard.*

And I get it: marriage is hard—that is a well-known fact—but it should not have been *this* hard, even on its worst days. Every day was a new struggle, struggling to get him to reveal his deeper emotions to me, to stay when we had an argument instead of taking off to parts unknown and not coming home, being kind and holding his tongue when he was angry and speaking to someone he loved.

"Love is patient. Love is kind. Love is not envious. It is not selfish or resentful. Love is rejoicing." Right?

These were life lessons I had already learned, and I simply did not want to tutor another person—at least not at the expense of my own emotional and psychological wellbeing. I was already so tired from everything that had happened to me so far, I doubted I could endure much more. It was giving me a permanent headache. I wanted to leave. As I would soon discover, the headache was not just from stress.

I was pregnant.

CHAPTER ELEVEN

CHAPTER ELEVEN

The First Daughter

When I found out I was pregnant, Marshall was out with some friends. I knew I hadn't been feeling well for a couple of weeks, and seeing as I had been through this once before, I decided to get tested. When the test came back positive, I felt conflicted. I had always wanted a home and more children, but this marriage was not going well. Quite frankly, it was exhausting. I felt emotionally abandoned, misunderstood, neglected. It wasn't exactly a lack of love. He had the ability to love. But our relationship was devoid of genuine attachment, complex emotions, and peaceful conflict resolution.

Marshall was a complicated man. Although he had a heart of gold, he had a severe withdraw with the respect to deep emotion and connections. My tendency is to search for the best in people regardless of how many times they hurt me. I now understand this a lack of boundaries. Back then, I thought I was doing the noble thing by loving someone unconditionally. If you are reading this, remember this about unconditional love: you must never lose yourself completely to heal another person, no matter their potential. They are the only person who can do that. If they are true-hearted, they will heal in their time. That is their journey. I repeat: do not lose yourself fixing someone else.

When I told Marshall the news, he was ecstatic. Conventionally speaking, we had created a comfortable life between Aaron and us. Aaron and Marshall had a wonderful bond that always made my heart smile. What I knew I needed more than anything for myself was for Aaron to be happy, and he had that now. In a few short months, there would be another baby on the way. I had already seen Marshall be a father figure, so I was confident this next phase would bring us nothing but happiness. Wrong again. Are you guys keeping score? (Please say, "No." Thank you.)

We found out we were having a little girl. I could not have been more excited! I would soon have a boy and a girl. That was what I always wanted. Unfortunately, I had a rough pregnancy. I was very lonely. Marshall and I were still so up and down; there would be a breakthrough, and then he would retreat into his shell, pushing me away. That wasn't what I wanted during this time.

If you're a woman who has ever gone through pregnancy, you know how you just want constant love and affection. You don't want to be fighting other battles you don't have the energy for when you can barely wake up and make yourself breakfast. I would cry so hard, I had to force myself to sleep because I didn't want to affect the baby. Things had gotten grim. I still felt love for him, though, and I hoped we could work it out for the sake of the children.

We had our little girl in February of 2018, a beautiful black-haired, brown-eyed angel. We will call her Mackenzie.

CHAPTER TWELVE

Mackenzie

I remember the day we took Mackenzie home from the hospital. There are a handful of moments in your life when you are flooded with absolute bliss. This was one of them. Aaron was so excited to be a big brother, and we were positive he would be the best one possible. He wanted to tell her all about the Avengers and teach her how to play swords. The day we brought her home, he sat on my lap and asked me why she was so small. I remember telling him, "She's just new here."

He laughed and said, "Yeah, we'll have to teach her a lot of stuff, huh, Mom!"

Yes, buddy, we will.

Unfortunately, the bliss didn't last long. I was exhausted, I was run down, and I had developed mastitis (a painful infection of the breast tissue) from nursing. I couldn't get Marshall to wake up during the night, no matter how many times I tried. I felt as if my body would give up on me. Worse yet, she was not sleeping because she had colic. I was running on about two and a half hours of sleep a night before I had to wake up and take Aaron to school.

For those unfamiliar, colic is the term doctors use when an

otherwise healthy baby screams intensely for hours for no apparent reason. I had already had Aaron and dealt with infancy, but Marshall was not prepared. This drove the wedge between us even deeper, and it would never be moved. I felt alone. I felt abandoned. I was tired, weak, and sick of pretending to be happy anymore. He was a loving dad—that much was evident—but I did all the backbreaking work with little support.

He didn't understand the hard stuff. I felt trapped because I couldn't even enjoy basic time to myself for even a moment because I was juggling so much. I knew I couldn't do it anymore, but honestly, I didn't know how to tell anyone. We jumped into this marriage head first because we were so head over heels in love, and I still loved him. I always would. Despite his faults, which we all have, he was kind, funny, and loving.

How did I explain to someone I wanted out when from the outside, I had made it look like I had everything? In the age of social media, you put on a sunny facade so that no matter how unhappy you are, you can be accepted. I was utterly lost and devastated.

A few of my closest friends had started to realize I wasn't acting like myself anymore. That fire for love I always had was gone. The girl who woke up dancing, ready to take on the day, was missing. The fire had gone out completely. I was just existing, taking it day by day with a smile on my face so my children would never have a clue.

Riese, his girlfriend, the kids, and I started spending a lot of time together. She was a godsend to me and would later become another sister I was blessed with. She loved Riese with all she had. She treated him with love and respect, as she did for everyone she encountered. She loved my kids and me. We loved her just as much. Mackenzie and Riese would come to form such a beautiful bond. The relationship reminded me of my own uncle, who helped raise me and was like a second father to me.

Mackenzie loved being near Riese. If there was a roomful of people, it was his lap she'd be on. They made each other laugh. He would text me every morning and ask how we were doing and ask for pictures of the kids. They were my biggest support network during that time.

It gave me the confidence I needed to start confiding in them about some of the things going on in my marriage. I trusted them because they loved us both equally, and not only were they invested in our wellbeing, but they were also highly educated in psychology and counseling. I knew they would be blunt with me. The things that flew out of my mouth shocked even me; I had not realized I had repressed so much sadness.

They lovingly told me that if we had both exhausted all our efforts to make it work when it clearly was not going well, we should amicably go our separate ways. I had a lot to think about. I wanted to present it in a way that would not hurt Marshall or give him any shame. He did not deserve that, and I did not want that for him. He had a lot to learn in life, and I had outgrown the exhausting situation.

We both knew it. We had endured too many life-altering challenges extremely fast. Whatever love remained would not be enough to keep the marriage functioning. Furthermore, after all the excessive, useless arguing, I was not sure if I was in love at all anymore. I spent the entire drive back to my hometown wondering what I would say and decided it was a conversation best left for another day.

CHAPTER THIRTEEN

The Accident

The events that happened next would change the core of my being. On November 13th, 2017, my world came to a crashing halt. I remember the day like it was yesterday.

Riese's girlfriend, Madison, called me and said, "Have you heard from your brother?"

I know, I said he was my cousin, but we always referred to ourselves as siblings. We were connected as if we were twins. We knew what the other was thinking the second something came out of someone's mouth in a room. We had spent every weekend together since we were kids and every day together each summer.

We were born five months apart and to different parents, but you know when someone is your twin. They will fight for you. They will understand every part of who you truly are. They know what to say and do when other people do not. Riese and I were this for each other. Twins separated at birth.

In our lives' darkest moments, we were there to hold each other's hand, metaphorically and literally. It is as if God gave us to each other as tools to get through this life. When we were little kids and he was scared and timid, I was fearless. I would reassure him everything would be okay and would feel his worries subside. As we got older, our roles would switch.

He was fearless. He dove head first into college and blew everyone's mind with his intelligence. Also a first-generation American and a product of two teen parents, he finished his bachelor's degree was, on his way to his master's degree and PhD shortly after. I, on the other hand, as an adult, would be lost at every turn, but there he was, holding my hand and reassuring me everything would be okay. I would figure it out eventually.

There was an ongoing joke between Madison and me. She would say, "Go get your brother. I can't talk any sense into him." The second I would walk into the room and see his grumpy face, we would both start laughing.

"You're kidding, right? Get up. You're being such a diva."

We would laugh and laugh. The twin relationship our souls shared was at the center of my being.

Back to the phone call.

Madison said, "Have you heard from your brother?"

"No, why?" I answered.

"He left work around three o'clock and told me he was running late for his class," Madison said. "He asked me to bring him lunch, and I haven't heard from him since."

My first thought was, *Hmm, that's not like him.*

As I mentioned earlier, Riese was a master of psychology, a master of communication, really. It was not like him to leave anyone unanswered, let alone Madison. I took a moment to think about how I wanted to respond because honestly, I was unsure what to say.

"Maybe his phone died," I said. "Have you checked back at the apartment?"

She reassured me she had been to the apartment, back to the college, and back to the apartment twice. This was not normal. I passed the phone to Marshall. He was much better at using the rational part of his brain rather than the emotional part.

I told her, "Here, talk to Marshall. I'm starting to panic a bit, and he's much better at handling these situations than I am."

I still do not know what they said. I remember Marshall pacing back and forth in the backyard. I remember staring out the back door and biting my fingernails, waiting for an answer. He came back in after a few moments and said, "She's going to search again and call us back."

I waited anxiously by the phone for what felt like hours. Exactly eleven minutes later, she called back and said, "I pulled his study buddy out of class. They were working on a big project together, and he knows it's not like Riese to not show up. He told me he hasn't seen him."

Panic.

I wanted to panic.

Madison and I are so similar. I knew if I panicked, she would panic as well, whatever she was doing to hold herself together. I took a deep breath and continued to pace around my bedroom. We decided to divide and conquer. She would call the police departments between home and where he was working, and I would call the hospitals.

I called two hospitals, gave them his name and birthdate, and asked if there was anyone there by that name. They assured me there was nobody who had been brought in by that name. For a split second, I gave myself hope.

Okay, he's not in the hospital, so he's probably fine! What's the worst-case scenario? His car broke down, and his phone died at the same time? Oh, man. He's going to be ticked if he has to walk in this weather.

It was so cold and rainy that day. Madison called me back and told me she also had been told he wasn't anywhere in the area as far as the police department was involved, which we figured.

It's been about an hour and a half, and no one had heard a thing. She had called my aunt, his mother, and let her know he hadn't come home from work or gone to class. People were posting about him on Facebook and saying, "If you see Riese, please call so-and-so."

Panic, now warranted.

Madison told me she and my aunt were going to drive the route he usually took from work to school to see if they could find anything. She assured me she would get ahold of me when they found him. I told her we would talk soon. My daughter still wasn't sleeping through the night, so I decided I would take a short nap. It was around seven o'clock, and my anxiety was getting the better of me, so I figured some rest would do me good.

They say that our bodies know when someone we have a close connection to is in danger. Call it a hunch, a sixth sense, whatever—I felt it that night. My heart wouldn't stop pounding. I couldn't wait to get a phone call and hear some sort of news that he was okay. I had no control over the situation, which was hard for me, so all I could do was nap.

Around eight o'clock, I finally heard my phone ring. I looked at the screen. It was Madison. *Thank God, they finally found him,* I thought.

"Where was he?"

"Amelia …"

"Yeah?"

"I need you to sit down."

Let me tell you something. When somebody you love with everything you are goes missing, someone who is so woven into the core of who you are hasn't been heard from in hours, and you are told to sit down, you know what to expect. You can feel it—a tugging at your heart, all the way to your soul. Naturally, after being told to sit down, I stood up.

"Why?

"Amelia, please sit down."

"No, just tell me what's going on."

My heart was racing. My feet had gone cold. I couldn't remember if I was still attached to the earth, but it didn't feel like it. I was a candle whose fire was about to be blown away by a storm.

"Riese is dead," she said as sweetly and calmly as she could.

I had known Madison long enough. I loved her enough to know she was the one who wanted to make that phone call to me. I wouldn't have handled the news well from anyone, but the way she handled things was full of grace and gentle intent. I don't know if she knows this, but I still admire how she handled that call. Her world was shattering too, but she put her feelings aside for a brief moment, knowing my lifelong twin, for all intents and purposes, was dead—and that I would not handle the news well.

I didn't know what to say. I wasn't sure why, but I thought it was some sort of sick prank. They had to have found him, and he thought it would be funny to pull this cruel joke. That's the only thing that made sense. He wasn't dead. He couldn't be! Not Riese! I finally remembered about gravity, and I collapsed to the floor without being aware of it. I dropped the phone and started walking up the stairs.

By now, Marshall had stopped what he was doing, realizing something had gone terribly wrong. He walked over to the phone I had dropped and picked it up, hearing the news for himself. I remember looking at him for validation. I was praying he would tell me it was, in fact, a cruel and unusual joke. Instead, I watched as he looked at me as if he knew I was about to have the biggest heartache of my lifetime, and that is saying a lot. He looked at me with heartbreak in his own eyes and stepped toward me. I stepped back onto the first stair.

"Please tell me they're joking."

He stepped toward me again.

I stepped back.

"They're joking, right?"

He took another step down.

I am not sure why, but I thought the bad news was attached to the phone. Maybe if I could stay clear of that phone, I could pretend it was not happening. He came closer, and I stepped back. That way, it would all be okay. Trauma is an unpredictable game. It alters your reality, making you react in ways you never would otherwise. One thing was for sure: I was not going to accept Riese was dead.

"No! Just stop! Stop coming toward me. Please, tell me they are joking. I need to hear they are joking. Please? Please?"

Silence.

"No ... no, please no. Please. Please, it's not true."

I was at the bottom of the stairs now. The only thing I could think to do was run to the bookshelf in the corner hide between it and the window. Make myself small, rest my back against the wall while falling to the ground, and scream. A crying scream so painful I was sure I shook the universe with it. I couldn't breathe. I couldn't think. I didn't want to move.

How could this be happening to me? Hadn't I been through enough in my life? Wasn't it enough I had grown up surrounded by violence? Wasn't it enough my other brother had drowned? Wasn't it enough I had failed in my dreams and aspirations by becoming a teen parent? The universe decided they had to take the one pure source of stability and support I had left.

There was that nausea again.

One thing I would come to discover about grief in the days, months, and years to come: it isn't linear. This started almost immediately. I don't know what I was overcome by, but I got up and started running down the street.

It doesn't make sense to you? It didn't to me, Me either.

But I did it. I ran and ran and ran.

I felt my body start to reattach to the earth for what felt like the first time in hours. My phone vibrated in my pocket. It was my mom. Let's rewind for a brief moment. I speak very highly of my mother now. We have done a lot of healing. She is a magically kind and well-tempered person. Well, now she is, but things weren't always that way, and I didn't want to speak to anyone. I answered the phone sobbing, and she said, "I just saw on Facebook. Riese is missing?"

I felt my adrenaline pumping. I knew he wasn't missing anymore. We knew where he was. I knew he was gone and I would never see him again in this lifetime. The reality was bleak.

I just heard myself say, sobbing, "Riese died, mom."

My mother, as special as she is, sometimes wears her heart on her sleeve a bit too much in moments like this. She just exclaimed, much louder than I needed to hear at that moment, "What?"

My parents were divorced at this time, but they had spent almost twenty-five years together, and she had watched us grow up together. Not only has she watched us grow up together, but she also played an integral part in it. We had spent most of our teenage years on our grandparents' property, which meant we had spent most of our teenage years around my mother's home. I could tell she was upset. I understood the news must have been devastating for her, too. However, my world had just crashed. Anyone who knew Riese and me could guess it would change who I would become for the rest of my life. As inconsiderate as it might sound, I didn't have the energy or the headspace to be letting anyone else in my headspace, so I hung up. I remember the air, mostly because I was still running, partly because there are things about a significant traumatic event you'll never forget. It was cold. It was early to mid-November, but it had already started to snow here in my hometown. I remember the rain drizzling on my cheeks. It was getting dark. Somehow, my body was hot. The news must have started circulating, because when I got home from my run, my best friend was at my house. I mentioned earlier that Jess, Spencer, Riese, and I were attached at the hip most of our teenage years and into adulthood.

Once Spencer wasn't around as much, though, the three of us remained each other's people. The early twenties were a chaotic mess for all three of us, if I'm being completely honest, so we found comfort in the small circle of the family we had created for ourselves.

She looked devastated—heartbroken for herself, for me, and probably for my whole family. Jess had been my best friend since childhood. My family was her family. She was standing on my front porch step when I walked up to her. I didn't say anything—neither of us did—but I melted into her arms and cried so hard I wasn't sure I would ever get back up.

We sat there for what felt like hours. Neither of us spoke. She just held me. I remember hearing her heartbeat, soft but fast. I could hear her sniffling. I remember she smelled like flowers and shampoo. Weird thing to remember, right? I would learn later that trauma activates the part of the brain located in the amygdala. Some people refer to it as the "emotional brain," which plays a primary role in our emotional responses. It turns out smells can be likened to those intense emotional memories. For the next year, I would hate the smell of floral perfume.

We eventually moved to the kitchen floor, where I finally stopped crying and looked at my phone. It had blown up. The news must have traveled—texts from friends and relatives telling me they loved me, people asking me if I was okay (why do people ask this, by the way?), others just saying they were there if I wanted to talk. Strange, but the text I kept frantically looking for would obviously never come. I wanted someone to tell me this wasn't real. They had made a mistake. Maybe someone had stolen his wallet and then got into an accident. There could be a chance they misidentified the body, couldn't there? Those things happened. Enter denial.

My phone rang. It was my aunt. I wasn't handling this well from the beginning, and hearing her voice only escalated that. My aunt is a petite woman, beautiful with a kind but stern voice. All I could muster was, "Please tell me it's not true."

She replied, "It's true, baby love."

"Are you sure?! Because they could've made a mistake. You know that happens sometimes!"

"There was no mistake, babe. It's him."

"Are you sure?" More sobbing. "Are you really sure?"

"I'm sure."

I let out a long, drawn-out, "No, please, no." My palm hit my forehead, my eyes closed, and I made myself small into the cabinet again and sobbed.

Jess had to go get her son, she told me she would come back if I needed anything, and she would be sleeping with her ringer on so I could reach her. It must have been the shock, but I don't remember saying anything back. I remember opening the door to my backyard and stepping out onto the grass. I hit my knees, sobbing so hard I was sure my esophagus would come up and I'd choke on it. I would up in the fetal position, wondering why God had let this happen to us. I know that was not the case, but it had always felt like we were all each other had. We understood the complicated things about each other and how to handle them. What was I going to do now?

I looked up at the stars. For a second, I thought how beautiful it must be where he's at. Was he looking at the same sky? Was he looking down at me through the stars? The universe is infinite. The possibilities are endless. Then I hit my next stage of grief, anger. Yes, they happen that fast. As I said, it's not linear. I could feel them all at once, two out of the three, one a day. It was never in sequence. I wanted him here, in my world. I had been through more than most up to this point in my life and was never one to throw myself a pity party, but I found myself at this moment wanting to call quits with everything.

I lay in the fetal position on the cold, wet grass, staring forward at nothing. I don't know if I was thinking anything or just existing. I heard the back door open up. It was Marshall. He came out and brought a coat to put over me. I had been running, sobbing, sitting outside for over two hours in just a tank top and leggings during November. As I mentioned, it had already started to snow where I lived. I never noticed I was cold until I was warm. I thought my body was incapable of creating any more tears, and then I would start sobbing again. I was refusing to go inside.

My sister had shown up and found her way outside with us. My body was so cold, she didn't know what else to do but lay next to me, giving me a hug in an attempt to warm my body up. Marshall would inevitably carry me inside, worried about my wellbeing.

When we got inside, Marshall sat me on the kitchen floor and beside me. My house smelled like goulash, and I remembered I had decided to try and make goulash in the crockpot for dinner for the first time that night. Goulash would be a meal I have not and will not make after that night. My sister, her boyfriend, Marshall, and I sat there in silence. This would be a reoccurring theme over the next few days. I did not mind, though. If you are religious, you know the story of Job. If you do not, that is fine too—I respect your choice either way—but let me explain:

Long story short, Job lives his life in a constant state of righteousness, so much so that God brags to Satan about Job's virtue. Satan swears Job is only faithful because he has been heavily favored. Satan asks God to allow him to test Job and see if he will still remain faithful. Within one day, Job receives news that his servants, his sheep, and all ten of his children have died. Satan continues to test Job, but his faith does not sway. Stay with me; it relates to the larger story. Job refuses to denounce God. What happens instead: three of Job's closest companions arrive to comfort him. They sit with him in silence for seven days while he grieves. Nobody knows what to say to me. What do you say?

See, the thing is, it's not always about the words. I learned more about my relationships during those moments of silence than ever before. They may not have known what to say to make me feel better, but they would be there. They would love my children in those few days when I didn't want to get out of bed.

Meals were brought. Friends I hadn't spoken to since high school called, texted, and wrote. People surprised me, in ways both good and bad. I lost some close relationships during this time as well. A hard truth about life is that sometimes when you're not the one keeping in contact, those relationships no longer flourish. It was an important lesson I needed to learn to move forward. I was so broken. I needed only the most supportive, most uplifting, lightest people in my life.

I was sitting wondering what I did to deserve all the pain I had endured thus far in my life. Had I angered God somewhere along the line? I must have been being punished for something because there is no way after the severe compound trauma that I had already experienced I would make it through this as well, especially when the one person I would need most to endure this hardship had been ripped away from me.

Now, I know Job didn't denounce God—I suppose I didn't either—but I was angry with him. I wanted to march right up there and ask him all the questions. Why my family? Why him? My grandmother on the same side of the family had been diagnosed with terminal cancer just months prior, and that had already shaken most of us. What kind of test was this? The God I had loved, served, and been faithful to had let me down, it seemed. Inevitably, I realized it wasn't my place to question the workings in place.

Whatever conflicted feelings I had about God at that moment, I knew I couldn't make it through the next few days without him.

I didn't sleep more than thirty or forty minutes the night Riese died. Neither did my aunt or Madison. I know because I texted both most of the night. I sent a text to my aunt that said,

> I know there's nothing I can say to you right now
> that's going to make this hurt any less. I know this
> because there's nothing anyone can say to me. Just
> know that I love you, and I'm here.

She replied almost instantly,

> I love you so much. I need you more than you know.

There were times during the night I could have sworn Riese was right there in the room with me, so close I thought that if I closed my eyes and reached my hand out, I could touch him. Not everyone believes in that sort of thing, but that's okay. It brought me comfort; that was what I felt. My heart was breaking into such tiny pieces, I didn't know if I could get up in the morning. I kept thinking about my family. How were we going to get through this? My grandmother was so ill, and I was so worried it would make her worse. Madison kept running through my mind. The love they shared was so inspiring. It was gentle, nurturing, understanding, forgiving, All the things you dream about in a connection, they had it.

No two grief experiences are alike. I was hurting, but it wasn't the same pain Madison was experiencing. It wasn't the same pain his mother was feeling losing a child. It wasn't the same pain his brother, dad, sisters, uncles, aunts, or grandparents would feel. Everyone has their own relationships, tailor-made from their individual experiences with another person. I knew, though, that Madison was broken. I prayed all night that God would give me the strength for the next morning, when I saw my family.

I hadn't seen anyone yet other than my sister, her boyfriend, my best friend, and Marshall. I didn't want to. I've done this thing my whole life where I walk into a room and try to put on a smile, no matter how I'm feeling. A mask so I never had to talk about the hard emotions written on my face. I had gotten so good at it, almost no one could tell how I was really feeling inside. (Alexa, play "homecoming queen?" by Kelsea Ballerini). "Do people assume you're always all right? Been so good at smiling most of your life." That was me, and I did not have the energy to do that at this phase in my life.

That morning, I got up, washed my face, and prepared myself to go face my family. I didn't know what to expect, but what I found was so much harder than I could have ever dreamed. When I pulled up to the driveway, my dad was just standing in the yard, literally just standing in the front yard.

That was different. As I said, I was prepared for anything in this situation. Our family was very close, and this would rock everyone's world. I walked up to him. I said, "Dad?" He looked at me. I could tell he had been crying. His eyes were light pink where it's supposed to be white. He gave me a hug and kissed me on the top of my head.

When I'm nervous or sad, I do this thing where my body just starts shaking. My hands tremble, my feet get hot, and I feel I am about to start an earthquake with my bare hands. I remember feeling quite vividly, but I couldn't cry.

I asked my dad, "Where's Madison?" He pointed to my aunt's car, parked in the yard, off of the driveway a bit.

"Okay."

I walked over to the car and saw Riese's oldest sister, my cousin, sitting in the driver's seat, but I didn't see Madison. I looked in the back seat, and Madison was curled up in the fetal position with her face buried in Riese's Green Bay Packers sweatshirt, which she was wearing. I knew this look all too well, as I had experienced it the night prior. Not knowing what to do to comfort her, I just laid right next to her, wrapped her in my arms, and let her cry.

The intense emotion must have been a turning point for my cousin as well, because she got out of the car, bunched up her fists, screamed at the top of her lungs, and started sobbing. My dad swept her up in a hug, and the four of us cried—separately but together. When we had regained our composure a moment, I walked into my grandmother's house and discovered the worst of it yet.

My cousin had graduated with his bachelor's degree from the university the year prior and had a professional photo taken. When I walked into my grandparent's house, I was hit with a sobbing no one should ever hear in their life. It was a sob of a mother who had just lost her baby. He was twenty-four years old, a grown man, but he would always be her baby. Earlier, I mentioned she had been a teenage mother. Riese was her world from the second he was born. Their bond was written in the stars and blessed by the heavens themselves, I was sure of it.

She was clinging to the photograph framed in a light-blue eight-by-ten frame. She was curled up in my other aunt's lap, simultaneously rocking back and forth, repeating, "Bring back my boy. Where's my boy? Not my boy. Bring him back to me." Exhale, followed by a long cry, a noise I cannot even explain. Repeat. Her hair was in a barely-there ponytail. She was supporting her CMU sweatshirt and black yoga pants.

I thought of her jeans—random, I know—but my aunt was a well-put-together woman who refused ever to leave her house unless she was wearing her work clothes or jeans. I don't know why these things go through your head when you're in a situation you weren't prepared for, but they do. Mine, at least. I was trying so hard to compose myself, I felt a lump in my throat so severe I couldn't swallow.

I quietly exited the living room, where my family was gathered and went out to my sister's Honda. I mentioned earlier I was never comfortable expressing my emotions in front of others. It was the only place there were no people, and it was parked off to the side away from other cars, so I knew nobody would find me. I opened the door, crawled in the back seat, and let out that scream once again, the one where you feel it with every fiber of your being. We've all had one. (If you haven't, 10/10 recommend.) It's the scream that comes when you're so broken that you don't know what to do other than release the pain into the universe and pray to God it never finds you again.

I sobbed and sobbed and sobbed some more. Then I heard the door open. My face was buried into the seat at this time, so I had no clue who it was and did not want to lift up my face, which I was sure was red, puffy, and gross. It wasn't who I was expecting. It was my sister's boyfriend.

He had a hard time fitting into our family because quite expressive mind of his own. Many didn't understand. I had known him since childhood, however, and knew his heart was soft. His intentions were usually well-directed, even if he didn't deliver them in the best way. He had known me since I was thirteen years old, so I can only assume he understood I didn't want to be touched or sat near because he opened the passenger seat on the opposite side of me, where I could hear his voice when he spoke, but we didn't have to make eye contact.

Silence. There it was again. I loved the quiet support. See, there was nothing anyone could say. I would probably get mad anyway. It was not anyone's fault. It wasn't my own shortcomings. It was just where my head and heart were at. I was in the anger phase of grief. That much was abundantly clear. I said, "It's not fair."

He replied, "No, it's not."

"He didn't deserve this!"

"You're right. He didn't."

"I'm so angry. So. Very. Angry."

"I know."

We sat there in silence for a few more moments until my sister came into the car. I don't know why. My sister and I are very close, but I pulled myself together and decided I would get up and go back inside.

The next few days were a blur. Every day I woke up, I felt as if I was in an alternate reality. It was rainy and cold, which didn't help. I was ignoring phone calls and messages. At one point, I pulled up a stool, sat at the window gazing with nothing really behind my eyes, and stared for almost three hours. I would go on walks by myself, listening to our favorite songs, silently grieving the life he should have had.

I thought about what he and Madison's wedding would have been like. They both played a big role in mine, and I was so looking forward to returning the favor. I wondered what their children would have looked like. How I would have spoiled them—fed them cupcakes and sent them back to the house hyper to run around and drive Riese and Madison insane. I mourned the world's loss because he had so much to offer. His brain was astonishing. His heart was pure. His only desire was to help people. I prayed for my family during these walks, as my keen sense of observation said my grandma had looked significantly worse yesterday. Then I would come home and go to sleep, hoping I would see him in my dreams.

The last time I had ever seen him alive was my son's birthday party, his tragic accident came just three days after Aaron's sixth birthday. Hard as I may try, that fact would cast a lasting shadow over future birthday parties.

CHAPTER FOURTEEN

The Viewing and the Funeral

I am a human who loves transparency. Since we're being fully transparent, since the moment I decided to write this memoir about my life, I have dreaded this chapter. I've written previous chapters with a pit in my stomach, knowing I was getting closer to this one specifically. I skipped past it and then came back with more writer's block. It was the darkest day of my life to date, and I prayed to God it would be my last on this earth. We're going to do this together, whoever you are.

The morning of the viewing, I woke up got into a fight with my dad because, well, who knows? I was angry, as I mentioned earlier. I screamed at him for asking what kind of Green Bay Packers shirts he should get because my family had decided to all wear them in honor of Riese. It was his favorite team, and he was a loyal Packers fan. Anyway, I screamed at him and told him I didn't have time to answer his dumb questions after literally asking him to get the shirts. Sweet, right? Told you. I'm a human who is fully transparent. I'm not proud of all my moments.

I hung up on him and sent him a nasty text (which I still regret to this day) and cried in my car. Today, I was channeling some serious anger I couldn't rein in. I could make sense of it, but I couldn't get it out of me in a positive way. It didn't excuse my behavior or the way I'd treated my dad, but I felt as if someone had taken a match and dropped it down my throat. I wasn't sure how to feel, think, or act. I did, however, later apologize for my behavior toward my dad. He was my comfort space, so I had dumped my feelings onto him, but it wasn't right. He was going through a lot too and didn't deserve to be my personal punching bag.

I got ready and headed to the funeral home.

I don't remember the beginning of the day …

I suffered through more than a day of writer's block after the sentence above. It appears my brain had completely blocked out the majority of that day until I sat down and really reprocessed it. Now that I remember it, I'm almost wishing I hadn't, but I promised you all complete transparency, and that's what I'm going to give you. This chapter may be a mess. It may be all over the place and hard to follow. If it is, I apologize. I just spent the last fifteen minutes in a ball on the floor crying, just remembering this day. But I will do my best.

Two days after Riese passed, my aunt asked me to put together some collages for his funeral. I spent a whole day going through photos and finding the perfect ones to honor him during his funeral. If there was anything positive that came out of this dark time, it was going through those photos. I was able to look at all the memories from the second he was born until the last few days on this earth. I got to see the big cheesy smile he had from the time he was a baby, over and over in every photo. I missed him.

When I walked into the funeral home, I wished the collage boards were the first thing I saw. Instead, my eyes immediately went to the casket. There he was. My aunt had decided on an open casket, so I am sure you can imagine the emotions that arose at that moment. The first few hours of the viewing were for close family only, so it was his immediate family on both sides, Madison, my aunts, and uncles. I purposely avoided looking at the casket. I had sworn I would not see him like that.

I walked over to my dad, who was seated a couple of rows back, off to the side. He gave me a one-armed hug, a kiss on the head, and said, "Have you gone up there yet?" I told him I had no desire to go up there and see him like that.

My grandma was in a wheelchair at this time, suffering from angiosarcoma, a rare form of cancer that was affecting her bones, so walking had become next to impossible for her. I remember looking up from where I had sat and saw her sitting all the way in the back of the funeral home. This resonated with me because, like her, I had no desire to be anywhere near that casket.

A few moments later, Riese's nana on his dad's side walked up and hugged me. We weren't directly related because she was his dad's mother, but I always loved her as if she was my own grandma—and she loved me back. Riese was her pride and joy. I was so immensely caught up in my own pain, it had slipped my mind into thinking about a few of the other people who adored Riese. He was so in awe of his nana. He loved everything she did. She is such a funny and warm woman; I swear, she has a talent for making everyone feel like family, which I always loved.

When she hugged me, though, I didn't feel any particular warmness from her that day, which is no surprise. None of us really had any idea what to do. I did, however, feel her slightly shaking, what I can only assume was a mixture of adrenaline and intense sadness. She, like me, refused to go up to the casket. In my mind, I thought, *Maybe we could do it together*. At least, I thought I said it in my mind. Apparently, I had said it out loud. I remember holding my hand out, she took it, and we walked forward.

I know someone else was with us at this time. I remember someone being on the right side, holding her other hand. I have been racking my brain for the last few minutes, trying to remember who it was, but I can't. Whoever you were, I love you. Thank you for being in that moment with us.

We were experiencing this together. I could feel her hand shaking in mine, or maybe it was a combination of the two, because I could feel my hand trembling as well. We walked up to the casket, and he looked so peaceful. He looked like he was asleep.

I have to stop here for a brief moment. Because I do not—nor will I ever—understand the concept of embalming a body, putting makeup on it, and having everyone that person loves most say goodbye in that way. You are more than welcome to disagree—I respect that—but this is my personal experience after seeing the human I had the closest bond with on this earth lying still in a casket, looking as if he could pop up at any moment and say, "Just kidding. I'm fine." It feels like exploiting a family in their most vulnerable moment. I am sure was not the original intent. As technology and resources emerge, so do the ideas people come up with to prolong the inevitable. Even if it means dressing up a corpse so their family can have that longed-for goodbye. I suppose I could see the appeal for some people. However, charging a family already in pain tens of thousands of dollars to say their final goodbye to a person they didn't want to die in the first place seems crass.

Back to the story.

Nana put her hand over her mouth and started really sobbing. I remember as we were walking up, she was half pulling back at every step. She knew she had to keep moving forward, but she didn't want to. Gravity was clearly the only thing keeping her connected to the earth. I didn't react how I thought I would. I felt numb. I don't remember externally having a response at all. I'm not sure what that was about. I suppose my brain was attempting to protect me from the severe pain I felt.

I looked at him and couldn't help but put my hand on his chest. I was hoping to feel his heart. I know it doesn't make sense. He was cold. I hated that. Symbolically speaking, it made no sense. He was the warmest person I had ever known.

He was buried in the same tux he had performed my wedding in, by the way, which was contributing to the extremely mixed emotions. I stared for a moment and walked away. I'm sure there are many more details about the viewing that I can't remember. As I stated earlier, I had writer's block just pulling this much out of my brain.

The few things I remember:

We all wore Green Bay attire to honor him.

My cousin, Madison, and I had bought green shoes to match our Green Bay shirts.

We were together as one force, supporting each other and getting through the day moment by moment, knowing that tomorrow, we would say our final goodbyes.

There was a brief moment of happiness where Marshall, my cousin, her boyfriend, and I were too overwhelmed by the heavy atmosphere this was the funeral home. We walked into the entrance, separated by two glass doors. There were two benches on each side of the walkway, and each of us took a seat. I don't remember now what was originally said. I just remember one of us said something, and all four of us burst out into uncontrollable laughter.

I'm sure if anyone saw us, they would not see our intense sadness. Home is where your family is, though, and we felt home—a brief glimmer of happiness.

The night before the funeral, I couldn't sleep. I kept tossing and turning. My stomach was in knots. My aunt and Madison asked me to give a eulogy I hadn't even started yet. Denial. Obviously, I knew what I would say. It was all in my brain. I had twenty-four years of memories with him, I knew the pain I was suffering and how my words could move the crowd that would be at the funeral, but I didn't want to write it. Why would I? Who ever wishes to write the eulogy for the person they loved most in this world other than their own children. Not me—that's for sure.

Eventually, I fell asleep. I woke up around 6:00 a.m.

Insomnia.

The day was going to bring on things I had never experienced thus far in my life, and my stomach was in knots. My body trembling started again. I figured since it was six in the morning and no one in the house was awake yet, I would start to write my eulogy.

I got out a pen and paper, sat staring at it, and the words were like a hurricane I couldn't get control of. They were spinning around in my head, yet I couldn't make sense of them. I couldn't figure out what I wanted to say. Maybe the problem was that I had too much to say, but I didn't want to say it to a crowd full of people. I wanted to say it to Riese.

It was then that it clicked with me. That is exactly how I would write it. I will write the eulogy as if I am speaking directly to him. Not the crowd. My final testament of love to my twin energy and best friend, the goodbye I was robbed of.

A couple of hours had passed. I got the kids dressed, got myself dressed in a long black dress, a black sweater, and black heels. Mourning. I normally enjoy dressing up. This was the worst experience with it I would ever have. The beautiful long black dress I had very carefully picked out of my mother-in-law's collection would be the first and last time I would ever touch it. Ironically, the sweater would later get a giant hole in it, I am still not sure where it came from, but I threw it away at the end of the night.

Mid-afternoon. The funeral is getting closer. I get in the car and drive to the funeral home. When I parked, Riese's dad would be the first person I saw. He and my aunt hadn't been together since they were teens, but he would always be my uncle. I remember bolting out of the car, running up, and wrapping my arms around him.

Riese looked a lot like the Filipino side of our family in the sense that he had thick black hair, the same olive tone skin color as I have, and dark eyes. He also looked strikingly similar to his dad in a lot of ways. They had the same build, gait, and ability to make a whole roomful of people laugh. Riese was infamous for his one-liners. He would say one thing that would tie together a whole entire conversation and leave everyone laughing. I cherished that about both of them.

We were there earlier than everyone else, just like the viewing.

It gave us time to come together in our grief and prepare. The first thing I remember was that I had bought green nail polish to paint the fingernails of anyone who wanted to honor Riese. I was surprised that I was painting not only the nails of most of my cousins, aunts, and others, but I was also painting everyone's nails—my uncle's, my dad's, Riese's friends' from college. I sat back there, maybe even avoiding the inevitable that was about to happen, but painting everyone's fingernails. We had some laughs, which seemed foreign at the time, but so right.

Whatever made us have happiness even for a split second was fine by me.

After I finished painting everyone's nails, I walked out into the main area of the funeral home. When I was about to pass the doors, I saw my aunt and uncle, who had traveled from Chicago. Riese and I had spent many of our family vacations with my aunt. She was always a breath of fresh air in our family. There were so many of us, strong-headed and stubborn, which made it easy for people to get trampled sometimes, but not her. She was strong. She had a strong sense of self. She would always take us to do fun activities, and the time we spent together was full of honesty, which Riese and I both admired.

She walked in the door, made a straight line right to me, put her arms out, and wrapped me in a hug. I could tell that she had been crying by her eyes. Seeing me seemed as though her heart was breaking more. I took a deep breath, trying not to cry.

It was time. The funeral was starting.

I sat in the front row with my two cousins (Riese's sisters), one on each side of me. My youngest cousin, seven, was cradling a teddy bear crying through her glasses. Riese adored all his sisters and would have been shattered to pieces. The image still haunts my mind. My older cousin was sitting to the right of me and was staring blankly ahead as I had been most of the day. We're a lot alike in that way.

Everyone was taking their seats.

The service started.

Before the service had started, I got a chance to look around the room. I can't say I am shocked at the impact Riese had because he was magic. He was bubbly, accompanied by a one-of-a-kind sense of humor and intellect. I was shocked, though, how many people had managed to make themselves fit into this funeral home. It was a big funeral home, the biggest one I had ever been in, and yet there were still people standing in every corner because there weren't enough seats. There were people standing by the door because they couldn't get in all the way. I remembered I had been asked to deliver the eulogy and felt my throat close up. I did not much care for being in the center of a room, let alone in my most vulnerable moment.

"I Can Only Imagine," by MercyMe. That was the first song to play. If you've ever heard it, you know it's an extremely powerful song. If you haven't, listen to it. All the heads in the front row from us family members went down into our hands, and we sobbed instantly. My cousin and I had lost it immediately, and I'd continue to keep my head in my hands for the remainder of the next few moments—until I heard my aunt start uncontrollably sobbing.

I mentioned my grandma was at the rear of the funeral home, in her wheelchair. She had asked to be wheeled up and grabbed my aunt's head in her lap. I don't remember the exact details, but I remember her telling her she was strong and could get through this. I recognized this because I had done the same thing to my grandma hours before the funeral, where she stroked my hair and told me to be strong. That's the gist; the details are a blur.

Everyone was crying. How could you not, even if you had just known us for a few moments—the love was as real as the pain, and you could feel it in the room.

We were trying to make it through. I blocked out everything the pastor said heard half of his uncle's eulogy, which was a beautifully worded, powerful poem. Collected bits and pieces of what Madison's said. I was going in and out of my consciousness, I think. Then I heard the phrase "has agreed to say a few words." I was zoned out. I can only assume now this was a defense mechanism. My brain wasn't going to accept this as a reality. My husband nudged me slightly, and I noticed the pastor was looking at me, waiting for me to come up. *Oh no.*

I stared at my feet the whole way up there. I could feel my heart pounding in my chest. I thought for sure I would throw up. When I got to the podium, I was surprised by my calmness. I looked around muttered, "Wow," awed by all the people who had come to pay their respects and grieve with us. I felt as if he were standing right there with me, holding on to my nerves until I made it through. I opened my folded sheet of paper and started reading. This is what I wrote:

> To my brother, my forever best friend. I love you more than I could ever put into words, and I'm grateful we told each other that every day because I never thought I would be saying goodbye to you. But I am so thankful because I have no regrets. We made so many memories and shared an unshakable bond. I have been so blessed to have been able to walk through this life by your side. Peanut butter and jelly. Spending our whole lives laughing, getting in trouble, creating memories, and protecting each other. I know you will grant me the strength to get through this so I can be there for our family and your precious Madison. That being said, I know you never want the circumstances that led us here to taint your legacy. You would want us to mourn. You always considered the feelings of others, and you understood that is important. But then you would want us to continue to thrive in our lives as you would. You were such a bright light that ignited a fire in everyone you met. You were sensationally brilliant, a man who loved fiercely and brought the gift of laughter daily into any given situation. Sometimes, even inappropriately placed, pushing

the joke as far as you could and loving every second because you knew your undeniable charm would prevent anyone from being upset. You were so much to so many people. You were a fiancé to Madison, and in her, I am grateful you found someone who loved you as much as I did, a second father to my children, a role model and lifelong angel to your residents, and the center of our family's universe. We will always spread your love and laughter to one another because that is the main root of who you are.

We will forever love and remember Riese. Let us live our very best lives as happy as we can because that is all he ever wanted.

When the funeral was over, the guests were asked to step out so the family could say their final goodbyes. At that moment, I laid my head on his chest and uncontrollably sobbed. My aunt said, "Come on, baby love. It's time." I refused to accept it. So did Madison. We both fought against it at this moment, absolutely desperate. She somehow found the strength to pull us both away from the casket. They lowered him and closed it. That is the last time I would ever see his earthly body.

The rest of the day are memories I have locked away in a vault I don't want to share.

Riese, we love you. We miss you.

CHAPTER FIFTEEN

The Cabin

My aunt and uncle from Chicago had rented a cabin on the lake not far from the funeral home. They had four small children and needed their own space while they were here. They bought pizza for everyone gathered. It was mostly our family and a few close family friends. Everyone had decided after the day we had we could use this time together. We were watching home videos. I heard one of my uncles say to the other,

"Who's that ugly guy?" when his face came on the screen

"Hey, that's Mr. Ugly to you."

We all chuckled. I really do love my family. In the face of adversity, which was a reoccurring theme in our lives, we were always able to come together and still laugh. We spent all spent the night just being in the company of one another. We played his favorite songs and danced. We told his stories and laughed so hard we couldn't catch our breath at times. We stayed up way too late reminiscing before we finally went to bed.

Madison, my oldest cousin, my two children, Marshall, and I pushed together two futon beds. We exchanged a moment where we acknowledged how grateful we still had each other, then crashed.

The next morning, everyone collected their things and headed in their opposite directions.

If you've ever intensely grieved the loss of a loved one, you're familiar with the idea of how unpredictable the days to come would be. Everyone had said the funeral would be the hardest day of my life. At the time, I thought that to be true. It was not. The hardest days of my life were the ones that followed. Everyone had gone home, gone back to work, forced to pick up the pieces and find our footing in the real world again. A big part of my world was missing.

Madison, Marshall, Riese, and I had a group chat we communicated in every day, vocalizing our struggles or triumphs of the day and playing the game crazy eights. We loved it; it had become the most supportive part of my life. Marshall was traveling four days a week, and I was always alone with the kids. It made me feel less lonely.

That was silent now. That deafening silence I spoke of earlier. I didn't enjoy it nearly as much now. I felt sadness, anger, denial, bargaining, depression, acceptance. Repeat. This would become a cycle for almost four weeks, until Thanksgiving. My aunt and uncle had come back again and rented another cabin so we could all be together. My grandma's cancer had gotten worse; she was looking much less like the strong, well-put-together woman I had always known and was looking much weaker. We all knew it was only a matter of time before we were saying goodbye to her too.

We had a great thanksgiving together. Everyone stayed the night in the five-bedroom cabin. We had breakfast in the morning and thanksgiving dinner at night. Riese's mom had brought that eight-by-ten photo of him as a memorial accompanied by candles. It wasn't the same as having him there, but it helped. I have native roots on my mom's side, so I have a strong sense of spirituality and felt he was there in spirit anyway.

My grandma was lying in the room because she couldn't move around much. We all gathered around the room in random chairs, around or on the bed, in the doorway—wherever we could fit—some of us coming and going or just spending those precious moments together. I had lain next to her for about an hour, listening to her talk. She kept telling us Riese was there, that she could see him.

I don't know what your beliefs are, but it's a widely known fact that for whatever reason, when people get close to passing, they start telling stories of seeing their deceased loved ones on the other side. It would come fast, and we needed to be prepared. This was barely six weeks since we had to bury my cousin. We were all just exhausted, taking it moment by moment.

A few days after Thanksgiving, I got a phone call. My grandma had taken a turn for the worst and was in the hospital. I went to visit her, expecting to say my final goodbyes. When I got there, her condition wasn't as bad as I had anticipated. She was, however, in a lot of pain, causing her to move around looking for comfort and moaning in pain. I hated that. This woman was fierce. She got diagnosed almost a year ago now, and they had told her then we should prepare for her to live no more than three months. She had surpassed that timeframe by nine months.

We got a few more days with my grandma. Then she passed away at home in her bed. She had come back from a doctor's appointment. My grandpa was out getting her medicine. My aunt was in the kitchen getting her something to drink. When she came into the room, she was gone.

I got the phone call, picked up my little brother, and rushed over there. When I pulled up, there were ambulances everywhere, and my grandpa was pacing the garage. My aunt was crushed. She and my grandma were each other's best friends. She had taken on the role of mother, caring for my grandma until the very end. They shot adrenaline in her chest and rushed her up to the hospital, where they prepared us to say our final goodbyes. She was all but gone, but the adrenaline had kept her heart beating. Once that stopped, so would her life.

My little brother is an angel on earth. He was different ever since his drowning accident but in the most amazing way. He was nineteen; mentally, however, he was more like a nine-year-old. But his heart was golden, he made us all better people. I had also not seen him cry since he was a baby. He was happy most of the time. When we walked into the room, his face went white. He started sweating and pacing. He was on the autism spectrum, so I knew when he started pacing behaviors, he was overstimulated.

I grabbed his hand, and we walked out the door. I said, "How are you feeling?" He tried talking to me, but his words were choked by emotion, and he started crying. I asked him if he wanted a hug. He said yes, then told me he wanted to go back in.

My cousins and my dad's other sister had shown up at this time. My younger cousin, closest in age to me other than Riese, walked in calmly. I was taken aback by her calm disposition because she was the closest to my grandma. They spent every day together while her mom was at work when she was young. She had been alongside her most of her cancer battle. She walked up next to the bed and started stroking her hair.

She was saying something in her ear that I didn't hear, or attempt to hear, allowing her that private moment. My dad lived in Indiana at the time and was rushing back as fast as he could. My heart was breaking because I knew he wouldn't make it in time to say goodbye.

I took a deep breath and sent a text asking him if he would like to say his goodbyes over Facetime because she would not live much longer. The only other time I had truly seen my dad cry was the morning of my brother's drowning accident. He was attempting to fight back the tears and losing that fight. His face shattered me. Pure agony was the only feeling I got from him. He wanted to be there; these are the defining moments that change our lives drastically. Once they're gone, you'll never get them back. He had to say goodbye to his mother over Facetime.

My grandfather was the last to say goodbye. He was holding her hand and telling us a story of when they met in the Philippines. A story I had never heard before. I had known this man my whole life and had never seen this side of him. He told her he loved her, and she flatlined moments later.

CHAPTER SIXTEEN

The Viewing and the Funeral—Again

Wondering yet why this book is called, *Don't Forget To Be Light*? It doesn't seem like there's much light about all the hardships we have endured as a family, does there? I read a quote once that said, "Grief is like the ocean. It's deep and dark and bigger than us all." I found during these monumental milestones in my story that while this may be true, grief may be as large as the ocean, but love is larger. It's infinite and everlasting, like the universe. It holds no limitations and yields to no one.

We grew closer in those two months than we ever had been. We spent almost every weekend together, the occasional weekday when we couldn't make it through on our own, support sleepovers, movie nights—you name it. That's where we found the light.

I'm going to make this chapter short because we had been through this process once, not even seven weeks ago, and in my opinion, the concept of a funeral is the same, regardless. They make me wildly uncomfortable.

The same group of us gathered at a different funeral home this time. This one was in my hometown, ironically, right across the street from my house. We put on our black shoes, dresses, shirts, and pants, once again to say goodbye to another pillar of our family. It was quiet agony that molded us together as one, so we could have the strength to stand against this relentless storm.

My sister spoke, Riese's sister spoke, all my dad's siblings sobbed. My cousin and I couldn't handle the amount of pain our parents were in and moved from our seats to the front row at our parents' feet.

We got through the day with tenacity and made it to the luncheon, where we were embraced by many of our family's oldest friends. That was nice, the moments we found solace in our shared company. If you were there and you're reading this, thank you on behalf of my whole family.

CHAPTER SEVENTEEN

Permanence

I had started to accept and process all the events that had affected my family in the previous two months. It was a whirlwind of bad news that picked up traction in an instant and didn't stop. I had to figure out how to move forward. I had two little kids—my reason for keeping it together. I was in school for early childhood development when Riese died. I always had dreams of becoming a teacher.

I stopped going to class after his accident just dropped out without even a thought of the consequences. Marshall had a respectable job, and we decided together it would not cause us any monetary turmoil if I just stayed at home with the kids while healing myself.

I would come to find out this was a big mistake. I should have been doing something for myself. I was giving myself the grace to get out of the house even if it was just going to class, going to the store, anything. However, I had two little kids and a husband who traveled for work most of the week. Even going to the grocery store was an uphill battle. If you are a stay-at-home mom, know that you are a superhero. Do not let anyone diminish your contributions. I would be doing that for the next two years, and I could barely keep up.

After my grandma passed away, we moved in with my grandpa to help keep him company and ensure he received the proper care. My grandma had been taking care of him for almost fifty years (I should know the exact amount, but I do not my apologies), a long time. Had we not moved in, he may have been living off candy and Campbell's soup out of the microwave. My grandpa had a sweet tooth, and Grandma always had to keep in check.

Five of us lived in a small three-bedroom, two-bathroom modular home. It was not easy, but we made it work until I found out I was pregnant. There was already a struggle for space, and as much as I wanted to be there for my grandpa, there was no extra room for another baby. We lived there for about a year before we bought our first home—an adorable ranch-style house on a corner lot in a subdivision.

I had never owned my own home before. I had not had a stable household growing up, and that was all I ever wanted for my family. I had thought it was the answer to all my dreams.

I enjoyed a few short months of blissful, stress-free pregnancy. For the first time in what felt like centuries, things appeared normal. I could start working on being happy again. I was due in March of 2020, and at the end of January, I got extremely sick. I had a headache so severe, I did not want to see any light or be around any noise. I could barely breathe. I felt razor blades in my chest every time I coughed. I spiked a fever of 103 but was freezing cold. I am almost positive I started hallucinating from the fever. I woke up from a dream and could have sworn someone was standing in my room.

I knew I needed to go to the ER. Something was wrong. I kept telling Marshall earlier that day, "I really feel like I'm going to die." He shrugged it off at first, and he insisted we go to the hospital once I started struggling to breathe. However, we all know how expensive American health care bills can be, and I did not want to go into the emergency room and spend hundreds, even thousands of dollars on them running tests, just to tell me I had a cold, so I waited it out. Late that night, I was struggling to breathe. Marshall was sleeping on the couch because we could not afford for him to get sick, too. I kept trying to scream for him, but nothing was came out of my mouth.

I managed to crawl out of bed and tell him I wanted to go to the emergency room. My face was flushed, but my cheeks were bright red from the fever. I looked terrible. I felt it too. They said it was the worst flu season they had experienced in years and had multiple people in with the same complications. She gave me tests for influenza and strep throat, both of which came back negative, but she said, "You look like the poster child for influenza." She gave me an inhaler, some Tamiflu, then sent me on my way. It would be two months later that COVID would run amuck and cause the entire world to shut down.

CHAPTER EIGHTEEN

The Pandemic

I was seven months pregnant, trying to fight off whatever this sickness was. It had been almost thirteen days, and I still barely had the energy to get up in the morning. My cough was slowly getting better, but I was constantly out of breath. My dad had come to visit us from Indiana for the weekend, my brother was also here, and they both got sick, ending up in the hospital testing negative for influenza. I remember my dad driving to my house and banging on the front door, asking me to take him to the emergency room because he was sure he was having a heart attack. He was clenching his chest and barely breathing. His wife had messaged me and said the night before he had a high fever and was hallucinating, swearing he was speaking to my grandma.

We got better in time, thank God. Then two months later, we would hear about COVID-19. I was sitting on my couch reading a news article about the people of Wuhan, China, contracting some unknown form of severe pneumonia in December of 2019. This would later be identified as the newest infectious disease, COVID-19, belonging to the SARS family of infectious diseases. Immediately, I thought of when my whole household had fallen ill with what seemed to be severe untraceable pneumonia.

I kept reading the article with curiosity and anxiousness. It told of the first confirmed case in the United States. I felt a pit in my stomach. It had run ramped in Wuhan, causing massive destruction and wiping out large portions of their population. The first American case was identified on January 20, and eleven days later, our president declared the outbreak a public-health emergency.

The first thing that ran through my mind was, *Whoa. I wonder if that's what we all had. It's here in the United States now.* My heart hurt for the impact it may make on the people of our country. I could not bear the thought of it wiping out substantial portions of our population. I may not have known them all, but they were my fellow Americans, and I loved them. The first few American deaths from COVID-19 would come shortly after, in February. I would check these numbers every day in horror. They were climbing so rapidly, doubling, then tripling, climbing as if driven by some unseen driving force.

All I could think of was my children. My unborn baby would be born with no immune system. During these initial stages of the pandemic, not much was known about how it was affecting children, but I had seen a few heartbreaking articles of young children falling fatally ill to the disease. My heart broke for their families and all the families swept up in the tragedy. They were not even allowed to say their last goodbyes to their loved ones; they could not even celebrate their lives with proper funerals, which were restricted to a handful of individuals.

I would often reflect on my individual experiences with death and grieving two years prior, thinking how we could not have made it through those challenging times without the intense support we found in each other. My mind would flashback to giving Riese's eulogy and finding comfort, even for a moment, seeing all the people who showed up to honor him, and knowing the impact on the lives he had encountered. I could not imagine being able to have that.

By the beginning of March, COVID-19 had spread to more than one hundred countries and was officially declared a pandemic.

I was due to give birth on March 16 and was terrified. I had watched the world come to a complete halt around me. Almost every state had implemented stay-at-home orders and quarantines to their people. I did not know what to expect.

My husband and I went to the hospital on the night of March 16 to be induced. I was having acute pain and discomfort with my hips and back, so the medical team decided this was the best course. They took our temperatures, had us put on masks, and sent us up. The nurse told me they were making my husband go home. A meeting had been called. Cases were skyrocketing everywhere, and no one could get the pandemic under control, so they were taking extreme measures. I instantly teared up. I told her, "I don't think I can do this alone."

I'd like to pause briefly and say to the women reading this book: if you had to endure childbirth alone during this pandemic, or—ever, for that matter—I am so sorry.

My husband had said, "I'm sorry, but I'm not leaving."

I was relieved because I was tired, worried, and did not have the energy to potentially be confrontational about the issue, but I knew I couldn't do it alone. She assured me she would double-check and come back. An hour later, my doctor told us she had already established she wasn't enforcing this rule because she didn't believe women should have to go through labor alone. I was so thankful for her. It was a long, hard birth, but sixteen hours later, on March 17, 2020, I had my second daughter—My St. Patrick's Day baby.

The moment I looked at her, I wanted to honor Riese by giving her his name. She had thick black hair and a button nose. I was so in love with her. I made her his namesake. We brought her home a day later, still unsure of the world she and the other kids would grow up in. It gave me anxiety, but for that night, at least, I was perfectly content.

We were quarantined for several more weeks. During this time, we were able to slow down and enjoy time with the kids as a whole family unit. It was nice. I felt guilty at certain times because we were some of the few lucky ones during this time. People around us were losing their jobs, losing their loved ones, getting sick, and we were being comfortable in our little bubble. Marshall had been allowed several weeks of paid time off, which helped integrate a newborn into the chaos.

He went back to work a few weeks later, and things got extremely intense.

CHAPTER NINETEEN

The Dark Years

The happiness I prayed would last forever was short-lived. Marshall was gone four and a half days out of the week. I was home taking care of two girls under two years old, one of whom was barely two months old, a toddler, and a school-aged child. We started fighting all the time. We never did it in front of the kids. We would never want to taint them. I had learned a lot from my childhood, the most important thing being I would never allow my children to feel when things were going bad for me, and they were going bad. We would fight over texts, in private, in our cars, in the basement, and he would leave and not come back. I learned to be strong, to stop sending that unreciprocated text, and to get some sleep. It might have been accompanied by a lot of tears first, but I would go to sleep.

We stopped fighting, mostly because we all but stopped talking altogether. He was sleeping on the couch, and I was sleeping in the bed, mostly with the girls. My middle daughter would always open the door around 5:00 a.m. and just come in and snuggle me. My kids were the only love I really needed right then. Most days, I ran around chasing my kids around and singlehandedly keeping the household together from sunup to sundown.

I would be so exhausted at the end of the day I would pray for a few moments of quiet alone time every day, and by the time I got a chance, my head would hit the pillow, and I would collapse into a deep sleep from exhaustion. I would sleep for two or three hours before one of the children would wake up, I'd get one of them back to sleep, and another would wake up.

I wasn't sleeping, I was barely eating, my health went into a steady decline. My heart ran at a glacial pace, barely making it from one beat to the next, and I felt it. I had distanced myself from everyone I loved and everything I enjoyed. I was ready to give up. The fire I had carried around inside me for years that made me passionate about life had completely burnt out. I felt like Poppy in trolls when she loses all hope, and all her vibrant pink body turns to grey. The only thing keeping me going was my children.

One morning, I stared at the pool in the back yard of my perfectly tailored subdivision life, thought seriously about what it would be like to drown myself in it, and realized I needed a change.

The thought was so intrusively real I messaged my doctor immediately. It was time to start being honest with myself and everyone around me. I would start there. I told her I had been struggling with extreme anxiety, stress, and depression. She prescribed me Zoloft, and the nurse I was speaking to kindly nudged me into the direction of some counselors if I wanted them for a resource, which I did. I would take all the help I could get.

We kept trying to make our marriage work at all costs. What I realize now is those "costs" were too high. We had lost the spark of the true love we originally had by trying to keep up with the facade of the perfectly put-together life. Polite, well-put-together children, house in the subdivision, the picture-perfect marriage—at the cost of who we really were. We had surrendered who we truly were to the complacency and conformity of society and lost what was profoundly important- our connection. Some life advice here; take it how it resonates: if you are not happy, *stop*. How had I not gotten the life-is-too-short memo from the numerous unexpected deaths in my family the previous few months? I am here now, though, to tell you: your happiness is crucial to the happiness of the world.

We had jumped on the bandwagon of the disturbed but slightly addicting Netflix serious, *You*. We found some comfort in our similar tastes in movies, at least. The more I watched the newest season, I noticed Love and Joe reminded me of us in a sense. Don't take this literally. Clearly, my husband and I were not homicidal maniacs. There was a message that resonated with me, though. There is a scene in which a friend says to her, "If there is ever, even for a fleeting moment, a tiny voice in your head, and that tiny voice is telling you, 'I deserve better,' listen to her. That's your partner."

Fireworks. It clicked with me. We were betraying ourselves, staying stagnant in something we both had outgrown. I loved Marshall, and I always would. He was a hard worker, he was a good dad, and he had a huge heart. As true as those things were, so was the fact we were no longer compatible. We did not enjoy the same things. We did not get along the majority of the time unless we were not speaking about anything deeper than the weather. It was a lack of any real connection.

I had started going to therapy to work through the years of trauma I had endured and clear out the junk folder of my subconsciousness. I continued to grow, change, and beg him to go to therapy so we could better understand each other. If nothing else, I wanted him to be able to build more meaningful, fulfilling relationships, not void of real connection. He also deserved a chance to speak to someone with an unbiased opinion about the things going on with him. Everyone deserves that.

I was constantly evolving. I loved that. The truth was, though, we were, as I said, outgrowing each other. The more we tried to make it work, the more we were changing ourselves into people who did that did not serve us authentically. I did not want that for him, either. However, I still wasn't ready to give up.

Who wants to give up on their marriage? You made a promise to this person, you made a promise to yourself, and you made a promise to God. I had made it abundantly clear to myself, though, that this marriage was no longer served my purpose on earth. Yet, I still refused to give up. Honestly, I was afraid of what everyone would think. I was a teenage parent, now we had two other children, and I was thinking about getting a divorce. The thought kept me awake at night. I had worked so hard to redeem myself from the mistakes of my past and was terrified that people around me would think less of me.

Then I came to a conclusion: Why do I care about opinions? They are just someone's thoughts. I do not have the right to control someone's thoughts. They deserve to think what they wish; it did not necessarily make it true. Especially when they did not have all the facts, and how could they? I was never honest about how my marriage was going.

I did not enjoy anyone knowing my business simply because I didn't want to hear the opinions. Although the truth is we pass by people every day whom we know nothing about. We sometimes feel entitled to give our opinions. Keep in mind, when you cross paths with someone, your first instinct is to form an uneducated opinion of them. Sometimes people are going through things they don't even feel comfortable sharing with their dearest loved ones. That's the problem with assumptions: we sometimes base our opinions of others on them. The problem with that is we mistake those assumptions as facts. More often than not, they're not facts.

Even when it comes to some of the most important people in my life, my initial understanding of them was completely wrong. This does not mean we ought to give a million chances to that ex who hurt you or that friend who stabbed you in the back. No one should have free range to roam through your life causing havoc. Don't blindly or quietly accept disrespect or malice, but keep your heart open to possibilities. Don't assume things about strangers based on a single encounter. Maybe you caught the nicest person in the room on the worst day of their life.

I read a quote a couple of months ago that said, "Walls keep people out. Boundaries show them where the door is." I thought that was so well written. Stop building the walls because the walls are built to keep people out, even the ones you need. Boundaries show you who is willing to live simultaneously in your life with kindness and respect.

We all know the phrase, "First impressions are important." Challenge yourself on that. Personally, I've found that it's the second, third, fourth impressions that are more accurate.

I started challenging myself to change my mindset on this. Instead of worrying about what the opinions around me were, I would worry first about myself and the happiness I desired. I wanted to tear the foundation of my mind down and start from scratch. What types of things did I find inspiration in? Where would I be my most authentic self? I decided I would go on a long, humbling journey of what would get me where I truly wanted to go in life.

It was uncomfortable. There is so much beauty and healing in growth. It is, however, uncomfortable. I had to accept I had developed behaviors I wasn't proud of; forming habits to change them would take time and practice. I started looking at everything as a challenge to show every person I came in contact with a smile and give them eye contact, even if just for a brief moment in passing. There has been so much negativity lately, and I wanted to be someone who would help change that.

I read many self-help books, listened to podcasts every day, turned off all social media outlets and gossipy magazine articles and news stories, and enrolled back in therapy. I learned more about the trauma from my childhood and how that affected my day-to-day life, including how I reacted to things. I had learned I had an intense fight or flight, which caused me to keep fighting for things long after they no longer served me. I learned about health, culture, religion, meditation, fitness, autism, and generational trauma. You name it, and I researched it, found a book, and bought it.

I wanted to have a better understanding of the humans around me and how I could help them. More importantly, how could I understand them? It was critical to me to understand the headspace people were in when they reacted to things, even if it was out of character. I had many of those moments in my life and wanted to allow people the grace to make mistakes, but I had to understand boundaries as well, because I didn't want to become a doormat.

I found a church in my hometown and started attending regularly. Here, I found a sense of home, family, and community. They literally saved my life. The first time I ever walked into the doors, I was showered with kindness. It was a big church, so I immediately got lost. The woman working at the welcome desk smiled and pointed me in the direction of the service. When I opened the door, I was in absolute awe. It was warm, there were neon lights on the stage, and they were playing live Gospel music. Music is the key to my heart. I stayed and listened to the angelic voices of the band. It was powerful. I didn't know what to expect from the message itself, though. I hadn't been raised around a church, specifically because my mom hadn't had good experiences growing up around them. I was pleasantly surprised, to say the least.

These people were inspirational. They delivered each message delicately, raw, and honestly. They covered topics dividing most churches. Mental health, LGBTQ+, marriage, divorce, remarriage—you name it. The pastor even did a whole series called "You Asked for It," in which he let the church members write what they wanted to talk most about, and he would cover it. Religion aside, this church would change the views of many people. The true, authentic message behind it all was, "Just be nice. Don't gossip. Talk with people, not about them, and love God."

After going for a couple of months, they mentioned one Sunday that they would be doing baptisms at their "church in the park" day. This was a large, three-service church, with more than a thousand attendees. The point of the church in the park was to get every person in one spot, at one time, to worship and spend time together as a family. I sat in my seat, thinking seriously about getting baptized. Then I chickened out.

The following Sunday, it was mentioned again. There was a testimonial video of a woman who had gotten baptized there a year prior, and her story truly amazed me. She spoke of how it changed her life, so I decided that day I would stop being a chicken and sign up. As I mentioned, I hadn't grown up in a church but had always wanted to be baptized and see my children receive the sacrament as well. So I signed up, invited some of the people closest to me, and went for it.

On August 22, 2021, I decided I would be baptized, giving full control of my life over to God, and be the best version of myself. The service started, and when it ended, they started talking about the Baptism and asking the people who had signed up to be baptized to meet them over by the tents they had set up by the river.

Aaron looked at me and said, "I want to do it, Mom." I was proud, but I wanted to assure him it was his decision, and I would not force him to do it. He said, "No, I want to!"

My dad and his wife were also there, and she turned to us and said, "Do you think it's too late for me to sign up, too?" I told her I was not sure, but we could certainly ask! They assured us both that she and Aaron could be baptized that day, if they desired.

The rest of the church gathered by the river. I remember feeling insanely nervous. I wasn't one for being in front of a crowd full of people, but I focused on the real reason I was there and was able to find some comfort in that. Aaron was clutching my hand because, much like me, he becomes anxious in front of a crowd as well, and neither of us knew what to expect.

When they called our names, Aaron and I walked waist-deep to meet the pastors in the river. They had a private few-second chat with us about how we were sure we wanted to give our life to God. The water was chilly, so Aaron and I giggled and quickly agreed. They had us link arms and dipped us back into the water. When we came back up, we heard our friends and family cheering, clapping, and looking excited for us. My stepmother was Baptized moments later.

I remember coming back out of the water. I felt immediately

refreshed, like when you take a sip of cool lemonade on a hot July day. I felt lighter. That night, when I went to bed, I prayed, thanking God for steering me in the direction of this church and the opportunity for my son and myself to be baptized. That night, while I slept, was the first time in as long as I could remember that I did not have nightmares. I did not dream at all, in fact, sleeping soundly through the night for the first time since I was a child.

I awoke the following day feeling loved and hopeful. I remember putting headphones in my ears and dancing around my bedroom, carefree for the first time in years. I did not feel I was carrying the normal weight of my anxieties, my life stresses, or what was coming next in my life. I just knew no matter what was to come next, I would be safe and protected. It was a complete 180°-turn from the stresses and hardships I had carried on my soul since childhood.

The music I previously liked did not sound the same to me anymore. Celebrity gossip, the news, certain movies, activities, and places did not bring me any true fulfillment anymore. I felt like whatever version of the woman I was before was shed in that water, and a new one emerged. Healthier and more excited for life.

A few nights later, I started having beautiful, ethereal dreams. Dreams of colors in sunsets I have never seen before, or at least not those shades of them, harmonious dreams where I would be sitting by a river in peace listening to the birds or walking in a field of flowers looking at nature. When I would wake up, I would remain attached to that harmony, and the weight of the material world did not feel as excruciating.

CHAPTER TWENTY

Applied Principles

I had all the knowledge and experience to make my life everything I wanted. Easy, huh? Not so much. No matter how enlightened we are, life will still tempt us daily. We still live in a material world where we encounter ugly things every day. I was tested big time with this during my son's football practice one day.

Aaron had intense asthma when the seasons changed. He was diagnosed with asthma when he was three years old and developed a cough we couldn't get to go away. There were nights when he would cough so hard, he'd make himself throw up. It was hard for him because he was such an active child, passionate about sports. He aspired to be in the NFL, so nothing would keep him from football practice.

Earlier that day, we had spent hours in the walk-in clinic following a flare-up. His regular doctor was swamped and couldn't get him in. Every other person in the town must have been sick on the same day because we spent three hours in there so we could get steroids and an inhaler refill for him. I politely asked him if he wanted to skip football practice considering how he was feeling, already having a pretty intuitive thought of the answer, which was, of course, no. He had missed football practice the day prior because, with COVID still running ramped, I wanted to make sure that wasn't what he had—and that he would not infect an entire football community.

I texted his coach to let him know he was in the clear; it was just his asthma. Gave him the note from the doctor and waited for football practice to get over. As we were getting ready to leave, his coach said, "How are you feeling?"

Aaron was struggling, coughing from asthma. Another mom, who I recognized but didn't know, had asked me if he was sick. I said, "He was sick as can be yesterday." Poor choice of words on my part, but I didn't think anything of it.

She looked personally offended and said, "If he's sick, he shouldn't be here." This pushed me back a bit.

I replied, "He's not sick. He was cleared by the doctor."

"What about the other kids on the team? He shouldn't be here if he's sick," she said.

It didn't matter what I would've said at this moment. I think she would've had a rebuttal, and I didn't want it to continue to escalate because Aaron was right there, and I could already feel he thought he did something wrong by being there, which he didn't.

The thought running through my head was, do you know me from somewhere and it not registering with me? Because I felt uncomfortable at that moment. As if we had crossed paths somewhere in our past and there were some personal feelings. It hit me: I recognized her from church. She got baptized the same time Aaron and I did. I said to her, "Do we go to the same church?" She looked mortified I had recognized her from a holy place after the recent confrontation. She said yes and reassured me her intentions were coming from working daily with children and was a firm believer kids in group settings should be kept home when they were ill. Understandable. I still did not appreciate the approach.

When we got in the car, Aaron kept asking me why he should not have been at football practice. I was agitated with the whole situation. I told him that because he was coughing, she might have been worried about her children on the team getting sick without realizing it was asthma which is not contagious. Aaron is a kind, understanding child, but he gets big feelings about things. He took it personally for a moment and asked if he should apologize to his friends for going to football practice. I told him no, he did not do anything wrong. Asthma is not contagious, as COVID is.

My mama bear instincts were in high gear, and I found myself frustrated for much of the night at the whole encounter. I thought, *You've been working for months on self-development and communication. You have all the tools to feel better about this situation. Just use them.*

I gave serious thought to getting her number, texting her, and letting her know I did not want to leave things on that foot. Could we go to coffee or something? But I was too nervous. What if I really was a person she just did not like for some reason? I did not think I could handle the rejection. I got her phone number from a mutual friend that we shared, just in case I decided to stop being a wimp and muster up the courage to text her. I prayed on it, and went to sleep.

Let me tell you what—God certainly has a sense of humor. I had a dream that woke me up at 4:00 a.m., when I was sleeping through the night for the first time in months about going to Sisterhood with her. Sisterhood is a ministry the church puts together where a large group of women come together, sing Gospel music, laugh, and do activities. I hadn't been yet, but I had wanted to go. I thought, *Why not? I'll text her and ask! The worst she can say is no.*

To my surprise, though, she replied excitedly, "I would love that! Thank you for the invite!" I felt good about this. I would later find out she didn't know I was the one who invited her; she just thought it was brave. I went to great lengths to get her phone number, and she wanted to go, as she hadn't been yet either. She looked shocked but excited when she walked through the doors to meet me and realized I was the woman from the other night. We exchanged apologies about the other night and the mutual thought that neither of us walked away from that conversation feeling good about it.

We sang Gospel songs together, spent an hour of sisterhood worship together, had a giggle about the first time we met, and exchanged a thank-you for being open to starting over and creating a new relationship out of the whole awkward affair. She gave me a hug and told me we should get together again soon, and we did. A new friendship emerged from the entire situation.

I had come to a crossroads. My life was changing. My mindset and ideas for what I wanted were no longer compatible with where I was at. I looked around my house. Marshall and I had worked so hard to get where we were at. We overcame many obstacles and built a comfortable life for ourselves. That was the problem, though: I have never been comfortable being complacent. I used to think it was a burden, confounded everyone except me seemed to have it all figured out. They knew exactly what they wanted out of life, and it was easy for them. I had struggled since the time I was a child with this.

People from my hometown had stayed and built beautiful families, opened businesses, and become teachers, nurses, and doctors. Some had left and never returned, taking on the world in their own respect. I admired it all. Mostly because I was so stuck, they inspired me. I always knew there was something different about me. I had tried it all—college, trade school, fitness, phlebotomy, stay-at-home mom, ABA therapy—all of it. I kept failing and failing, then failing some more.

However, as I mentioned earlier, the good news about life is that you learn so much more from your failures than you do from your successes. Then, if you have enough failures and learn from them, success will surely follow. So, I looked around my house, thought seriously about getting an apartment that day, and moving out. Certainly, it would not be the right thing to do. The people who loved me deserved more respect and honesty than that. Marshall and I had been separated for about three months but hadn't told any of our friends and family with hopes to rekindle the marriage.

It hit me that day: it wasn't going to happen. The root of the issues at hand were not being addressed. I waited until he came home on Thursday. We sat at the table and talked. My heart was breaking looking at this person with whom I had spent so many years. He was a great person, and I knew this would hurt us both, but we had to start being honest with ourselves. He took the news it was time to file for divorce with humility. He was good at that. He had a composure in emotional situations about him that helped me learn many things about myself and life. For that, I will always be grateful.

I allowed myself to mourn silently. I started waking up in the morning and listening to meditation. I bought what seemed like hundreds of candles so my house would smell nice and be the atmosphere I would need to support my next journey. I had mindful meditation and subliminal positive affirmations playing into my ears from the second I woke up until the second I went to sleep. Literally everyone who was around at this time can attest to this. I was conscious about the food I was putting into my body and the thoughts going through my mind. I started waking up at 5:30 every morning to work out before the children woke up. As I previously stated, it was uncomfortable—but I could be temporarily uncomfortable or permanently stuck, and that was no longer an option.

My sister was living with us at the time we split. She had been going through a rough time that year, as were most people. Struggling to find work, she had lost her apartment, so we moved her and my niece into the spare bedroom in our basement. My sister was a strikingly beautiful woman. The only way I can even think to describe her is a mix between Esmerelda (the Gypsy from the *Hunchback of Notre Dame*) and Tinkerbell. Seriously. She was much like my grandma in the sense that she stood five feet nothing, with tiny fairy hands and feet and the voice of an angel. She had been blessed with a singing voice that shook me to my core.

She was one of the biggest support systems at this time. She helped make sure my children and I were taken care of while I ran around like a chicken with my head cut off, writing this book. Headphones in all day, listening to mindful meditation messages so nothing would seep into my subconscious and distract me from my goal. At the end of each exhausting day, we would cry, laugh, and sing passionately at the top of our lungs. Then we would wake up the next day and do it all over again. We would dance unapologetically around the house, blasting "Show Yourself" from *Frozen 2* and "Hallelujah" by Pentatonix. The kids absolutely thrived in this situation. I realized if I am genuinely happy, my kids would follow suit, a lesson I truly needed to learn, because their happiness being tainted was my biggest concern about deciding to divorce in the first place.

Marshall was gone during the weeks, and I was staying with friends during the weekends so we didn't disrupt the children's comfortable environment. I was all but living out of my back seat from Friday to Sunday. I remember I had so many clothes in the trunk of my SUV they would fall out when I opened it for anything. I was doing my makeup out of a plastic Meijer bag and carrying my laptop around so I could write it all down and finish my book.

If there was a visual embodiment of support. I felt it at this time. Only a few close friends and our family knew we were going through a divorce. I was private about my life thus far, and I enjoyed that. We were loved, and everyone just wanted us to be supported and the best for us. The people who did know were nothing short of angels and helped me out in every way they could. Madison had just moved in with her boyfriend. Three years after the accident, she had finally healed her heart and found happiness. Similar to Riese, she's a soft-hearted woman, so it only made sense she would attract someone like that.

He barely knew me, and they hadn't lived together long, so they could have easily asked me to respect that time in their lives, and I would have. They didn't, though. They took me in on the weekends, making the spare bedroom as comfortable as they could so I had a sense of home. My dad, who was remarried, and his wife took me in a lot during these times as well, giving me the respect and privacy I deeply craved while offering their silent support. My mom would come and stay with me to help with the children even though she wasn't sure what new project I was up to.

No one other than my sister even knew I was writing a book. I was too busy absorbing the things around me like a sponge, taking mental notes of everything, wondering how I could make a positive change through my experiences, inspired by the people around me. Life had been hard for many people over the last two years, not just within my family but as a collective society, and I wanted us to work together to change the world. I believed we could, or at the very least, realistically make a large dent.

I just had to find the words.

I was constantly taking out my phone, writing everything down. Half the time, it didn't even make sense, and when I didn't have my phone, I wrote it down on any scrap of paper I could find. The inspiration was there. I was ignited like a fire. God had been waiting for me to let loose. I was shaking all day, every day with excitement and adrenaline, not allowing the fear of rejection into my mind because I had no choice but to do this. I had given in and given it all up to the fate I was sure God had created for me. Faith.

Marshall and I sat down and amicably discussed how we would split our assets in the divorce. I didn't want to enter a long, drawn-out legal battle fighting over something that would only damage us both further and put our kids in the middle of something ugly. I wanted him to have the stability and courage to go forward in nothing but calm. I took all the pictures off the walls because that's all I wanted to take with me—and maybe the couch. I was fully confident in my abilities to become successful and buy another home if the situation arose. I would only be able to do that if I was putting out only positivity into the world in hopes some of it would be returned.

One night, it all became too much. It was like a pot boiling all over, leaking down the stove, cabinets, and floor that was my life. Our lives are made up of a million little pieces, floating around us like matter floating in the galaxy, just waiting for us to connect the dots, but before you connect those dots, it's just messy and confusing. That's why people refer to the moment of truth. It's not beautiful all the time. Some of it is really dark and ugly—I know from experience. I've had moments in my life so ugly I wanted to hang my head in shame and never show myself to the world again, moments so painful I was sure I would break right along with my heart. This was one of them.

I asked Madison if I could come to see her and gave her very little explanation. As usual, she said, "Come on down!" She had barely opened the door before I made my way to her couch, melted into a puddle, and couldn't stop sobbing. Her boyfriend walked out sweetly, looked at us, and said, "I'll go grab the wine."

He offered his support by bringing us every snack in the house, making a beautiful charcuterie board filled with deli meats, cheeses, jam, you name it. He brought me tissues. Then went into the room to respect my privacy, even though I hadn't asked him to. I could not like him more if I tried. He was a genuine all-around person whom Madison had conjured up straight out of her dreams. We talked for a while, shared some tears, and she told me, "I can't wait to see where you're at in six months."

It gave me the inspiration to keep going when all I wanted to do was lay on the floor and die, watching the walls of the life I had so meticulously built burn around me. I missed my children. I missed my family being together. I was dreaming of the beginning phase of my marriage before we let the messy world get the rest of us. I was lost, confused, and downright exhausted. I remember wondering if it would get better in time. Or, like many other things in my life, would I have to learn to live with it?

My heart was breaking in every sense.

The next day, I decided I would wake up early, put some positive affirmation tunes on, and meditate. I had been reading books and articles written by Dr. Joe Dispenza about the ways meditation can change your life. I watched an interview with him where he said, "It's a scientific fact that the hormones of stress down regulate genes and create diseases, long term effects on human beings because of the size of the neocortex and its ability to turn on the stress hormone by our thoughts alone. That means our thoughts can literally make us sick." Then he said, "Is it possible, then, that our thoughts can make us well?"

Wow.

I did more research based on his evidence-based science linking meditation to positive health effects on the human body and decided I would start meditating every morning. Forcing my body to sit and work through my thoughts and break sets of behaviors I had formed through the years of trauma. Joe Dispenza had said, "The way we experience the world is highly subjective." He was right. If I could just rewire my brain to see the positive in things, my life would change. Yes, I was going through an extreme life-altering transformation. It didn't have to be a bad thing, though. They say the most beautiful flowers bloom in adversity, and I was determined to use this time to bloom.

I sat out on the front porch of Madison's apartment, which overlooked some stunning natural scenery. I drank coffee and let out a gut-wrenching cry. Then a cardinal came and landed on the tree directly in front of me.

This was extremely symbolic for me, because shortly after Riese passed, I saw them everywhere. Many of the people in my family were. Someone told us when you see a cardinal, this means you are receiving a visit from a loved one in heaven and that they show up when you most need them or miss them. An article I once read stated they appear during times of celebration as well as despair to let you know they will always be with you.

I took this as a sign everything would eventually be okay.

I didn't know how.

I didn't know when.

I had faith it would, though.

I got dressed and took Aaron to a trampoline park, where we bonded over these moments. We jumped with light hearts and joy.

We had some funny conversations. It was a breath of fresh air. When we were leaving, he said to me, "Mom, I have a question."

I replied, "Okay?"

"Would you rather be poor and have your family around you, or would you rather live in a big mansion all by yourself?"

What a philosophically appropriate question.

I thought about it for a moment and replied, "Hmmm ... I would way rather be poor and surrounded by my family. What would be the point of having all that money if you had no one to share it with?"

"True. You could always get a dog."

We both laughed.

CHAPTER TWENTY-ONE

Sisterhood

Thursday came around again.

I would always get a pit in my stomach because regardless of my drive or where my mind was at, this had been my home for several years, and it deeply pained me to leave. Thankfully, though, Sisterhood was that night. I had every intention to go, originally, until those random waves of emotions came over me, and I went back into hermit mode. I thought, *No, I don't want to go be uplifted right now. I want to sit with these emotions and process them. That's all I want.*

A few minutes later, I checked my phone and had a text from my friend. I mentioned her earlier, the football mom who agreed to go to Sisterhood with me two months prior. She said, "Sisterhood tonight?"

If you're anything like me, you look for signs in small signs you're on the right track. I had asked her to go last month, and she was unavailable. I found irony in the fact she would text me today, so I switched my mindset, got in the shower, asked my dad and his wife to watch the kids, and left.

It was the most ethereal experience I have ever experienced in my life. I'd been attending that church for almost seven months, and I'd had some monumentally moving moments. This didn't compare. Every song was sung directly correlated to something I had experienced. Some of the lyrics in the songs I had literally said out loud during this last week. They were moving and powerful. The energy was magnetic. We threw our hands in the air and gave it all to God. It was exactly what I needed.

When it came to a close, the lead singer of the women's worship team came out and addressed the crowd. She was visibly shaken and started tearing up. It looked as she was staring directly at me and said something along the lines of, "Someone here is going through something incredibly heavy. I have felt it all night. Please, if this is you, come up to the front and let us pray over you. The prayer team will be upfront waiting for you."

What? Did that really just happen?

I mentioned earlier my crippling anxiety about expressing my emotions, let alone to strangers. I was going through a divorce, which I wasn't sure they would agree with in the first place. I didn't want to be judged. I sat on it, grabbed my coat, and prepared to leave. My whole body felt heavier, as if bricks were weighing me down. I knew I had to release this weight to someone, but I was scared. I said aloud without thinking, "I'm pretty sure they were talking to me."

Remember, at this time, *no one* knew what was going on with me. If you had looked at my Facebook, you would have seen a picture of a perfect life. Literally. My friend kind of looked confused. She said, "Okay, let's go then!" I took a step back and started stuttering, "No, ehhhh, No. I don't think so. I can't. Never mind." I started anxiously giggling, another tick I have. She was strong. I could tell that about her the first time I ever met her. It probably intimidated or rubbed certain people the wrong way. I know it did to me at first. She was kind, though; I could tell by the way she lived her life. Words aren't everything, mostly because many people don't know how to use them correctly and every person has a different vocabulary and their own interpretation of certain words, even those technically speaking the same language. You can't always trust words.

Back to the point. I needed that strength, and God put her in my path with that night written out in his plan—I am sure of it. She grabbed my hand and marched me up there. She put her right arm over my opposite shoulder and offered enough support to let me know she wouldn't leave me during that time. I was shaking uncontrollably, probably because I was trying my hardest not to cry even though my body knew it needed to release those emotions.

They asked me what was going on. I had my eyes closed, but only word vomit came out. I thought I would just spill about the divorce and let them pray I get through it with some grace and dignity. Instead, twenty-seven years of trauma-induced word-vomit came out, everything from the alcohol and drug induced abuse in my childhood, the drowning, the teenage pregnancy, the two deaths, the funerals, then the divorce.

Poor girl. She looked up at me in horror, but not in the way you'd think. More like, "How are you still standing?" Also, said friend and I barely knew each other, so she started tearing up hearing it for the first time.

The woman on the prayer team didn't even know where to start. She said, "Okay. I don't want to minimalize any of what you just said. But what are your specific wishes for this prayer?"

I said, "I just want prayer for healing and to get through this with grace." She started praying for me, and with my eyes closed, I could only describe this experience as the physicality of guardian angels. Someone had their hand on my back, someone was holding my hand, there was a person who had put their hand on the back of my head, and when they were finished, I burst into tears. It felt as though I would be okay for the first time … maybe ever.

The energy was so powerful, we all just started hugging. My friend and I walked out of the church. I thanked her for being with me during that time. We hugged one more time, and then I went home. I slept soundly that night for the first time in over three years.

CHAPTER TWENTY-TWO

The Phoenix

The next few months of my life would be the most challenging I had ever endured. (I keep saying that, don't I?)

I continued to wake up every day and meditate, clear out my negative thoughts, re-process all the things I had been through, and feed myself only positive thoughts. I could have easily been angry at the way my life was going, but the thing is, anger is just like cancer inside your body. It will keep multiplying itself and spreading like wildfire if you don't get control of it. It will leak out onto people that don't deserve it and create a universal shift through an extension we don't need.

Over those few weeks, I barely spoke to anyone. I was protecting the energy I allowed around me like an animal with survival instincts. I stayed up hours on end writing and editing my book. I would wake up at three in the morning with ideas popping into my head and write them down. See, the thing about those thoughts that pop into our minds: they're seeds. If we water them, they will become the most beautifully abundant tree of fruit you have ever seen. Trust me.

I had seventy-seven dollars in my bank account and was living off faith and a dream, literally. I went to use my credit card for gas, and my card was denied due to insufficient funds. Marshall would never have cut me off financially until I got on my feet. He was not that kind of person. He was kind and understood I had sacrificed a lot, including my career, to make sure the kids and home were cared for. I had to do this without him through, and I knew that. I needed to exercise my ability to independently make my dreams a reality and express my creative gift to the world.

Thirty-three days after I started writing my book, I had finally reached the last chapter. I reflected back on the eye-opening life shift I had just endured and allowed myself to be in awe of my determination and resiliency. I had become a fighter in every sense of the word. Not violently or literally, a fighter, but a fighter about things that mattered to me. I learned to stand up for myself in situations that made me uncomfortable and steer conversations away from negativity or gossip. I had allowed myself to speak my truth with love and authenticity, which people respected. I changed the dynamics of my relationships because my cup was overflowing with so much love it was rubbing off on those around me, and that was what I was most proud of.

I went to the store, gathered all the supplies I needed to put my book together, and sent it out to publishing companies, praying I would hear something back. I put together a box of a manuscript and some pictures of my family so whoever was reading about them could picture their faces. I prayed over it, took it to the post office, and waited.

A couple weeks later, I still hadn't heard anything. I was feeling a little defeated and thought, *Maybe I'll just call the publishing company?* I got nervous and hung up the first time. Then I realized I would never get anywhere if I lacked the courage to make a phone call to a publishing company, so I called back. The publishing company I had sent my package to told me they were not currently accepting admissions, and I felt my heartbreak. I was so excited, so sure that was my path. Immediately I felt discouraged.

I thought for a second about giving up, going back to my normal life, and finding a nine-to-five job that was comfortable and secure.

Then I felt an undeniable nudge to open my phone and just type "Find a publisher." Immediately, a helpful website came up asking the right questions. "What type of book? What are your long-term goals?" I hadn't really given much thought to the "category" my book would be, so I typed in "Testimonial," and based on this, they directed me to a publishing company called WestBow Press. I figured, *I've come this far. I'll give it a shot.*

I called the number and waited anxiously. After almost eight rings, a man picked up. I said, "I don't know if I'm even on the right track here, but I wrote a book. It's really good, and I believe it will bring a lot of good, but I have no idea what to do next." Don't know where that came from. Me and my word vomit.

He kind of almost giggled and then started explaining to me that he was the senior publishing consultant and the publishing team lead. Also, how ironic it is that I even caught him because he is hard to get ahold of. He explained they were committed to presenting positive and inspirational Christian messages.

I started laughing. "Perfect!"

We had a great chat for almost thirty-five minutes about the ironies of God's work. He said something to me I will never forget. "God will only nudge us on the shoulder so many times before he starts throwing bricks at us."

I knew right then I was on the right track. He told me I caught him at the perfect time because they were at the end of the biggest publishing promotion of the year. I told him all about my book, the inspiration, and the story behind it. He was intrigued and decided he would help me get my book published.

After I got off the phone, I was clenching so hard to my steering wheel, feeling like I might pass out. I started sobbing with relief. I had done it. I had conquered every trial, tribulation, and hardship, coming out the other end better for it. The sun was shining on my face, and I felt God's light all around me. He moved the mountains out of my way and paved a clear path.

Ironically, the first person I wanted to call was Marshall. So I did.

He picked up the phone and lovingly exclaimed, "I'm so proud of you, Amelia."

Later that week, he asked if he could take me to dinner to celebrate. I agreed. We sat with no regard for the past or future. We let the present wash over the conversation and let it flow. We sat there for what seemed like hours talking, laughing, and getting glimpses of the new people we had both emerged from the previous several months since we split. I felt at complete peace. We exchanged goodnights and went our separate ways.

Over the next few weeks, we slowly started chatting more. He would ask me about my book's progression, and I would inquire about his work endeavors. We would laugh over things the children did during the day. He startled me one day by telling me he had been going to therapy and asked if I would be comfortable hearing about some of the things he had discovered about himself, which of course, I always enjoyed learning more about.

Five months after the initial split, and ironically, one month before our first appearance to the court for our divorce, he asked me if I would be willing to go away with him for the weekend to celebrate my birthday, to which I agreed. In the car ride there, we blasted music singing along. At dinner, we laughed until our stomachs ached. And at the end of the night, we engaged in hours of deep, meaningful conversation. That void of meaningful connection was gone. He was my biggest supporter, and I was his. God had led us on a humbling, five-month journey where we learned crucial lessons, and ensured we would found our way back together.

Where is my journey taking me next? I don't know. None of us really do. We can only take it in strides, as Rascal Flatts would say, "Find God's grace in every mistake, and always give more than you take." Allow yourself the courage to find your most authentic place in the world, whatever that means to you. I truly pray for peace and love for whoever finds this book. That was the original intent behind me writing it. It's not a sob story of every harrowing experience life has thrown my way. I wanted it to be an example to you all: if I can do it, you can do it too.

Your untapped potential is inside of you, patiently waiting for you to decide what comes next. Even if that just means you decide you'll forgive your parents, make the phone call to that friend you're at odds with. Stand up for yourself in that conversation that keeps coming up. Whatever it is, I pray you take it in strides. Believe in yourself, and those around you.

Know that if you played any part in my journey, the good, the bad, or the ugly, you have helped me grow into the person I am today. I am proud of her, and I hope you are too. I have wished you all happiness from afar.

My best advice for a happy life? Keep an eye on those around you. Do that thing that terrifies you. If you have fear standing in your way, burn it to the ground and do it anyway. You are more powerful than you think. You play an integral part of this beautifully woven world we're all a part of. God has a plan for us all—if we listen closely.

As love was told in *You* by her friend, "If you ever, even for a second, hear a voice telling you deserve better, listen to it. That's your partner." Don't abandon our true-life partner, yourself. You have one life; you deserve to make the most out of it.

You can make a home anywhere. Home is where your people are. And believe it or not, we are all each other's people in this life. If we treat each person as an extension of ourselves, we may just be brave enough to see the world change in front of our very eyes.

Love unapologetically, break the social norms around you, and don't forget to be light.

Love you,
Amelia.

LET THE CREDITS ROLL!

Music inspiration for this book:

"Half of my Hometown," Kelsey Ballerini
"True Colors," *Trolls*, Justin Timberlake/Anna Kenderick
"Show Yourself," *Frozen 2*, Idina Menzel/ Evan Rachel Wood
"Reflection"—Mulan Soundtrack—Lea Salonga
"Tell Me How Long," Kristen Bell
"Even If," MercyMe
"I Can Only Imagine," MercyMe
"Rose Tea," Curtis Roach/Kynzi
"Hallelujah," Pentatonix
"homecoming queen?" Kelsea Ballerini
"Amazing Grace," Carrie Underwood
"Weary Traveler," Jordan St. Cyr
"Goodness of God," Rhett Walker/Essential Worship
"Rest For Your Soul," Austin French
"Landslide," Glee Cast
"A Broken Wing," Martina McBride
"See You When I See You," Jason Aldean
"I'll Be Missing You," Puff Daddy/Faith Evans
"My Wish," Rascal Flatts
"So Small," Carrie Underwood

"I Hope You Dance," Lee Anne Womack
"I Wanna Dance with Somebody," Whitney Houston
"Hope," Twista/Faith Evans
"The story," Jana Kramer
"Cheering you on," KING&COUNTRY
"Hold on," Justin Bieber

I pray whoever finds this book is inspired and has as much faith in it as I do.

Disclaimer:
All names, locations, and dates have been altered for the sake of privacy.

This is for my family.

Sincerely,

Amelia Homewood.

Printed in the United States
by Baker & Taylor Publisher Services